WITNESS
TO HISTORY

WITNESS TO HISTORY

RECOLLECTIONS OF A WORLD WAR II PHOTOGRAPHER

ROBERT HOPKINS

Castle
Pacific
Publishing

Castle Pacific Publishing Company
Seattle, Washington
Washington, D.C.
www.castlepacific.com
Printed in the United States of America

ISBN 0-9653869-4-5
Library of Congress Catalog Card Number 2002 141509

Dedication

Acknowledgments

I am deeply grateful to my friend Robert Wister, Professor of Church History at Seton Hall University, for his patience and the care with which he proofread the text of this book. His scholarship, corrections and comments sharpened the focus and improved the cohesion of this account of World War II.

Useful also has been the contribution by Fred P. Crouch, who was born more than two decades after me, and who correctly pointed out that terms familiar to me during World War II were no longer in the vocabulary of the younger generation and required amplification. I incorporated these and other useful suggestions from him in my final draft, with my heartfelt thanks.

I admire the skillful work done by Abby Cadle who made high quality reproductions of the photographs I took during World War II. I am beholden to her for her cheerful dedication to this task.

Finally, I am mindful of the patience and forbearance of my wife, Brenda, who endured days and nights of loneliness while I was engrossed in writing my wartime memories. She experienced more than her share of the conflict from 1940 to the end of the war when she survived the intense day and night bombings of London by the Nazis. Her memories of the terror, turmoil, destruction and wanton killings are those she wishes to forget.

CONTENTS

INTRODUCTION

Eminent scholars and historians have written volumes about World War II, so it would seem there is little left to reveal. But because of the momentous events which occurred in my lifetime and the special access I had to world leaders who shaped those events, there remains more to be told.

I knew President Franklin D. Roosevelt because my father, Harry L. Hopkins, was his friend and advisor, having worked closely with him as administrator of the Works Progress Administration (WPA) during the Great Depression, as secretary of commerce, and as director of the Lend-Lease program during World War II. Fortunately for me, I had the opportunity to be with the president and his family repeatedly in the years which followed.

As a U.S. Army Signal Corps combat cameraman in the European Theater of Operations from 1942 to 1945, I filmed the Allied invasions of North Africa, Italy and Normandy, as well as many of the ensuing battles.

I also served as President Roosevelt's official photographer at the wartime conferences at Casablanca, Cairo, Teheran and Yalta. When Roosevelt met with King Farouk, Emperor Haile Selassie and King Abdul Aziz ibn Saud in separate meetings in the Suez Canal, I was there and photographed those encounters. Upon President Truman's return from the Potsdam Conference, I photographed his meeting with King George VI aboard the HMS *Renown* in Plymouth Harbor, England. Finally, in London, I filmed the victory celebrations marking the end of the war in Europe and in Japan.

The films I made and the photographs I took, along with those of other army motion picture cameramen and photographers, form the official U.S. Army pictorial record of World War II.

Now, more than a half-century after World War II, few people are alive who were present at the deliberations of Allied leaders and who also experienced the realities of war. I was one of those. I was not a policy-maker or a military strategist. I can claim no credit for the decisions reached. But I knew President Roosevelt, Prime Minister Churchill, Marshal Stalin and their principal advisors. Because I was often with them at informal gatherings and meals when they were at their ease, I believe I can relate aspects of their personalities which have not yet appeared in histories of this era.

Roosevelt, Churchill and Stalin, the prime movers in the war against Nazi Germany, shared as an essential element in their alliance the determination to defeat Hitler and wipe Naziism from the face of the earth forever. But each held basic, unshakable post-war convictions which tempered their relations with one another.

Roosevelt believed and declared that to achieve lasting peace, liberated countries everywhere in the world should be independent and their governments elected by the free will of their citizens. Furthermore, all should enjoy the right to freedom from want, freedom from fear, freedom of expression and freedom of religion.

Churchill, however, was an ardent champion of colonialism—the source of England's strength—which imposed the will of the Crown on the governments of the countries it had conquered. I was present on at least two occasions when Churchill promoted the idea of an English-speaking union, which seemed to me to be an effort to incorporate the United States into the British sphere of influence.

Stalin was determined to prevent Poland from ever again becoming a welcome mat for invading armies into Russia. His country had been invaded too often at the cost of millions of Russian lives. It was this determination which prompted him to negotiate the ill-fated Russian-German Non-Aggression Pact with Adolph Hitler. Only when the war ended was Stalin's hidden agenda revealed to extend and expand communism throughout Europe and the world.

When Allied leaders met to discuss strategies during World War II, they were influenced by these convictions, by the pressures of war, and by their ability to meet the challenges they faced. Working with these factors they determined a course of action which they fervently hoped would lead to victory and a lasting peace. Some historians, however, who lived to see what ensued have found it hard to resist the temptation to be judgmental of the decisions reached.

For example, after Roosevelt died of a cerebral hemorrhage six weeks after the Yalta Conference, newspaper and magazine editors thumbed through the photographs I took at the conference and printed the one or two in which the president looked weary and drawn, while they passed over those taken seconds before or after in which he appeared presidential, relaxed and good-humored. This prompted political analysts to surmise that he was so sick at Yalta that he made bad decisions. Later, some historians stressed the same theme. The president was certainly tired on that last day of the Yalta Conference, but this was not a precursor the cerebral hemorrhage which struck without warning. From my own observations of the president that day, I can state that he was highly satisfied with the agreements reached at Yalta.

The pictures I took during the war years are among those which illustrate this book. They, my diaries, and my wartime letters carefully preserved by my parents and my wife served to sharpen my memory of the events described herein.

CHAPTER 1

EARLY ENCOUNTERS
WITH PRESIDENT ROOSEVELT

I was fifteen years old when I first met President Roosevelt in 1936. The occasion was the president's inauguration of the Triborough Bridge in New York. Below the bridge, Randall's Island Stadium—which was built by the Works Progress Administration (WPA)—was to be dedicated in the same ceremony by my father, Harry L. Hopkins, who headed the WPA. He arranged for me to ride with him in the presidential caravan up Fifth Avenue.

The president rode in a car ahead with the top down. It was an exciting, stimulating experience. The caravan was flanked by a score of escort policemen mounted on motorcycles with side cars. Their roaring engines and flashing red lights added to the excitement. Huge, enthusiastic crowds lined both sides of the avenue. Confetti and streamers showered down on us from the windows of buildings above.

We stopped off at 65th Street so the president could visit briefly with his mother who lived there. Dad and I accompanied him. I was dismayed to see that he was carried upstairs by two Secret Service men. It was only then that I realized the president of the United States could not walk.

I was introduced to the president's mother, Sara Delano Roosevelt. She seemed to be a stern and dominant woman who doted on her son. As she brushed confetti from his shoulders, she scolded him because he was not wearing a sweater. He protested that it was a warm day. She persisted and took a sweater from the cupboard and handed it to him. He obediently put it on.

I was on the speakers' platform with my father and I took my first pictures of the president there with my fold-out Kodak camera. I had no inkling that I would photograph him hundreds of times in the future in far-off exotic lands.

After the speeches inaugurating the bridge and the stadium, the president left and returned to Washington. My father and I stayed on and watched the Olympic trials held that day in the stadium and witnessed Jesse Owens break the world's record for the 100-meter dash—a prelude to his remarkable performance at the Olympic Games in Berlin later that year.

In 1939, my younger brother Stephen and I were on our summer vacation with Dad at Delabrooke, a house in Maryland right on the Patuxent River where Dad was recuperating from a serious illness. On July 5th he told us that the president was going to visit us that day, and that he would arrive at six o'clock in the afternoon aboard the presidential yacht, *Potomac*. We would do some fishing, then have supper on board. Stephen and I, and my half-sister Diana, watched eagerly from the widow's walk as the yacht appeared around a bend in the river at exactly six o'clock. A Chris-Craft speedboat, piloted by a Secret Service man, picked us up and took us across the water to the yacht.

The president greeted us on deck. He was casually dressed in sports clothes and wore a floppy white cloth hat to protect him from the sun. He was accompanied by a tall attractive woman who he introduced to us as Crown Princess Martha of Norway. With her was her daughter, Princess Ragnhild, a youngster about Diana's age. The two girls ran off together to explore the yacht.

As the *Potomac* got underway to take us to fishing grounds in the Chesapeake Bay, the president told Dad stories about goings-on in Washington and they joked together while Crown Princess Martha stood by smiling at their exchanges. While he was aboard the *Potomac,* the president seemed to shed any concerns he may have had about the disturbing events in Hitler's Germany or political problems at home .

We dropped anchor and fishing poles and lines were brought out, a pole each for the president and Dad. The princess did not fish, but made herself comfortable in a wicker armchair near the president. The president gave Stephen and me a line each. He instructed us on how to bait the hook and how to drop the weighted line to the bottom where the fish would be biting. He told us to yank up the line as soon as we felt a nibble. He made it sound easy.

Secret Service men, manning two Chris-Crafts some distance off, slowly circled the yacht while we fished. I had plenty of nibbles and my bait was repeatedly stolen, but I didn't catch a single fish. My father and my brother were also unlucky. The president, however, caught six.

It was growing dark on that warm evening when we put away the fishing gear and the Filipino mess boys set up supper for us on deck. The captain raised the anchor and we headed back up the Patuxent River while we ate our supper to the gentle motion of the yacht.

Off-shore from Delabrooke, we took our leave of the princess and her daughter, and thanked the president for that wonderful adventure. We then skimmed back to the landing at Delabrooke aboard the speedboat.

After I graduated from prep school in 1940, I received the following handwritten letter from my father. I was puzzled that it was written on White House stationary.

THE WHITE HOUSE
WASHINGTON

June 7, 1940

My Dear Robert,

I regret more than I can tell you that I cannot be with you on the day of your graduation. I remember so well the day of my own graduation from high school and the thrill that comes from passing one of the important milestones of life. That was in 1908 and I was beginning to face, as are you, the next adventure. And I was happy, untroubled, unafraid. That was easy to do then, it is not so easy today. For the world is in turmoil. The forces that are now unleashed will cause profound changes not only in our economic life but in your own personal way of living thru the years to come. Already you must have made a deep searching of your heart and mind. What is the true meaning of this terrible and almost unbelievable conflict in Europe? Does it have a significance beyond the age old struggle for power? Can this country remain aloof from its impact? In what way can it affect our personal lives?

You and I, think now perhaps for the first time, of the meaning and importance of those freedoms that make a democracy different from other national political systems. The right to choose your own friends—to speak and think without restraint—to share in whatever religious life gives you deep and abiding satisfaction—to dwell on the surface of the earth as freemen, one with the other. I believe that in these things lie all that is important and good in life. I am equally sure they are in danger—grave danger—from forces that represent the very antithesis of those things we hold dear. And you and I must decide whether these freedoms are worth fighting for—whether in war or peace, this conflict is upon us. And we shall win not only because of our physical strength but if our will is strong and indomitable.

Life has had some minor tragedies for you but to this point it has been a happy and joyous experience. And I know you have lived it well. You have courage, strength and a clean spirit. And above all you are unafraid.

I shall think of you on graduation day with a warm heart and ever so proudly.

With all my love,
Your father, H.L.H.

I had attended a prep school in Massachusetts—Mount Hermon—which was founded in the late 19th century by Dwight L. Moody, an evangelist preacher. My classmates and I followed the war in Europe with lively interest, but visiting lecturers were all either pacifists or isolationists who downplayed the gravity of the situation. I was 18 when I graduated and I knew I had some serious decisions to make.

On May 10th, less than a month before my father wrote this letter, the president had invited him to supper at the White House. Hitler's armies had thundered through Belgium, Holland and Luxembourg, and were poised to invade France; Neville Chamberlain had resigned and had been replaced by Winston Churchill as prime minister of England.

The president and my father talked deep into the night, measuring the impact of these dramatic developments on the United States. Long past midnight, the president asked my father to stay overnight so they could review incoming cables and dispatches in the morning. He put my father up in the Lincoln Bedroom. The following morning, the cable traffic was so heavy and significant that the president asked him to stay on so they could deal with it together.

In fact, my father stayed on in the Lincoln Bedroom of the White House for three and a half years, using it both as his bedroom and his office where a card table served as his desk. His move into the White House explained why my graduation letter was written on White House letterhead.

When my father became a permanent guest at the White House, Mrs. Roosevelt insisted that he bring his daughter Diana with him, her mother having died three years before. Diana was given a bedroom on the third floor, above the Oval Study.

I think the president and Mrs. Roosevelt, their own children having grown up and married, enjoyed having young people around.

After Dad moved into the White House, I was a frequent guest there, spending weekends and holidays with him. I slept in the sitting room adjoining the Lincoln Bedroom at the southeast corner of the White House. I had to get up early because the sitting room also served as the office for my father's secretary. The windows looked out on the South Lawn and the Washington Monument. When I returned from the war and saw the magnolia tree that President Truman had planted there, I could not help but think that tree must have ruined the view from the Lincoln suite.

I was told that President Lincoln's ghost walked through the rooms and corridors of the White House in the still of the night, lamenting the terrible loss of American lives in the Civil War, but I never heard or encountered him.

Mrs. Roosevelt was particularly kind to me and welcomed me to the White House almost as if I were a member of her family. Whenever she was not away on one of her frequent trips around the country, she and I had breakfast together in the Blue Room downstairs. It was Mrs. Roosevelt who taught me to drink coffee for breakfast instead of milk, breaking me in slowly by offering me cafe au lait and serving me decreasing amounts of milk on successive days.

She talked to me candidly on these occasions when we were alone. She told me it troubled her deeply that her children could not commit themselves to one spouse for life, but divorced and remarried repeatedly. She said that whenever they married, she welcomed the new wife or husband to the family circle and was genuinely fond of several of them. This was particularly true of Faye Emerson, Elliott's wife, and she maintained their friendship long after Faye and Elliott were divorced.

Mrs. Roosevelt knew that my mother and father divorced in 1930 after 17 years of marriage. Although she made no direct reference to it, I think this was her gentle way of urging me to make my marriage, whenever it occurred, a lifetime commitment. I had already made that promise to myself, remembering how hurt I was when my parents parted.

There was something old-fashioned about Mrs. Roosevelt. She was the mistress of ceremonies at all family parties, for example, and set the theme for them in advance. I was present at one of President Roosevelt's birthday parties. Mrs. Roosevelt had decreed that the theme of the party should reflect her husband's tenure as assistant secretary of the navy and that all gifts should relate to that. At an antiques shop my father found two prints of ships of that era. He had them framed and gave them to the president.

At my father's birthday on August 17th, Mrs. Roosevelt decided the theme should be Abraham Lincoln because of my father's admiration for Lincoln and because he was resident in the Lincoln Bedroom. On this occasion, the president gave him a copy of a fascinating book entitled "Lincoln Talks," which according to the editor contained a collection of verbatim conversations Lincoln had with various people.

My father particularly treasured another gift from the president—a pair of gold cufflinks each bearing the engraved initials HLH on one side and FDR on the other, denoting their closeness with one another. Thus, he became a member of the "Cufflinks Club" composed of a half-dozen of the president's closest associates. In each case the recipient's initials were engraved on one half of the link and Roosevelt's on the other.

The intimacy of the Roosevelt family was notable by the nicknames they used with one another. The president called his wife "Babs" and his daughter "Sis." Anna's two children, Eleanor and Curtis, were dubbed "Sistie" and "Buzzy," nicknames they discarded as soon as they were old enough to assert themselves. Elliott addressed his father as "Pop." Roosevelt's personal secretary, Marguerite LeHand, was called "Missy" by the president. Nicknames were also used widely among close associates of both Roosevelt and Churchill, and I have indicated these wherever appropriate.

As close as my father was to the president, I never heard him address him other than "Mr. President." To my knowledge, Felix Frankfurter was the only one, aside from Mrs. Roosevelt, who called him by his first name.

In the evenings I came to know the president when he relaxed after dealing with the affairs of state. He took an interest in my studies and in my ideas for the future. He guided me in the books I read. During the war, when I covered the Big Three Conferences, the president made sure that I was invited to the dinners attended by Allied leaders.

The introduction of Robert Hopkins into the U.S. Army on October 7, 1941.

I often walked Fala, the president's scotty, on the South Lawn, but I became conscious of tourists staring at us through the iron fence as if we were creatures in a zoo. Thereafter, I walked Fala in a less conspicuous part of the gardens.

On one occasion when my younger brother Stephen and I were visiting my father together, the president invited us to join him for a swim in the White House pool. Here, every day, Admiral Ross

McIntire, the president's doctor, massaged the president's legs underwater in a vain effort to stimulate their nerves and muscles. Despite his infirmity, the president was strong swimmer. He had powerful shoulder and arm muscles, and played a vigorous game of water polo with us.

I expected the White House—as the center of power of the United States—to be a busy place, with telephones ringing incessantly and secretaries hurrying along the corridor, carrying sheafs of documents. But this was not so. It was a quiet place very much like any private home, although considerably larger.

Next to my father's room was the Monroe Treaty Room, which in those days was a catch-all for unused furniture. It was dominated by a massive billiard table over which hung an out-sized crystal chandelier. Mrs. Roosevelt told me that her uncle, President Teddy Roosevelt, had taken a fancy to the chandelier and had it brought over from the Capitol.

The long east-west corridor on the second floor was lined with bookshelves filled with mystery books, which the president enjoyed reading. Archibald MacLeish, the Librarian of Congress, saw to it that the latest mysteries were there for the president.

The president's daily routine rarely varied. He would have breakfast in bed while reading the newspapers, embassy cables, dispatches and memoranda. He was joined by my father and they determined which matters needed immediate attention. The president turned some of these over to my father for action.

Then, after Arthur Prettyman helped him get dressed, the president would heave himself into a simple armless wheelchair and lift his legs, one at a time, to the footrest. When the president was settled in his chair, Arthur wheeled him to his office in the Oval Study, where his desk was cluttered with brass donkeys, ship models and other mementos given to him by friends. There he would settle down for his day's work.

It was the president himself who designed this wheelchair using, as a point of departure, a straight-backed oak chair from the kitchen. He had a board bolted to the front legs to serve as a footrest, then he had 6-inch wheels attached to the legs. Those on the front wheels had swivels for steering.

The president rarely called a cabinet meeting, preferring to meet with cabinet members individually or in groups of two or three to deal with specific problems. During my visits to the White House from the Spring of 1940 until the Fall of 1942, there were no official dinners. The last one, a state dinner, had been held in 1939 for the visit of the king and queen of England.

In the evening, the president would mix and serve cocktails, invariably dry martinis, to his close friends. Mrs. Roosevelt didn't approve of drinking and did not attend. Then the president would invite Missy LeHand and Dad to a simple supper prepared by Mrs. Nesbitt, the housekeeper. After supper, the president would either work on his stamps or invite friends like Sam Rosenman and Ben Cohen to join them for a game of poker. Sometimes Mr. West, the Chief Usher, would set up a film projector at the east end of the corridor and we would watch one of the latest films from Hollywood. The president usually turned in at about ten o'clock.

In May 1941, I was twenty years old and had just completed my freshman year at the University of North Carolina. I had landed a summer job in New York City at *The March of Time*, a documentary film subsidiary of Time Incorporated.

I was hired as a research assistant at $25 a week plus any overtime I accrued. My job was to verify the facts in the film scripts prior to production and to attend showings of the films at Radio City with script in hand to record audience reaction at appropriate parts of the script. Whenever I had time, I observed the other aspects of film production.

A 15-minute *March of Time* film on current events was produced every two weeks. It was a hectic schedule and I found myself working day and night, doubling my salary with overtime. These films were shown in theaters throughout the country immediately prior to the feature film. They were popular and influential. They were produced by Louis de Rochement with a small staff of only ten people, including secretaries.

I worked on eight or ten films including "Texas Under Seven Flags," in which I made the embarrassing error of attaching the wrong date to the fall of the Alamo; "The German-American Bund," during which I accompanied the film crew when the FBI raided Bund headquarters on 86th Street; and a film about the saga of four Norwegian flyers who crossed the North Atlantic in a small sailboat, were picked up by a U.S. submarine, then joined the Canadian air force contingent which became part of the British Royal Air Force (RAF) for the defense of London during the Blitz.

In the five months that I worked for *The March of Time*, I felt that I was learning far more than I learned at college and, because the film unit was so small, I absorbed a good deal of information on how documentary films were produced. I decided that I would not return to college, but make documentary filming my career.

I discussed this with Louis de Rochement. He told me that the U.S. Army was just forming a film unit in the Signal Corps at Fort Monmouth in New Jersey, and that Hollywood directors, writers, cameramen, actors and technicians who had been called up in the draft were flocking to join it. He said that because I was underage and would not be called up for another year, I could volunteer for the army now and designate my preference to join the Signal Corps film unit and be assigned there. Working with the best professionals from Hollywood, I would get first-rate training in film-making.

I talked to my mother and father about this and pointed out how important this move could be to my career. My mother wanted me to continue with college, but finally relented when she realized I would be called up before I finished my college education. My father was enthusiastic about the idea. With their approval, I volunteered for the army and enlisted as a private at $21 dollars a month on October 7, 1941.

Army public relations got wind of the fact that I was joining up and as I was being processed a number of reporters and photographers descended on me and there was a flurry of stories about me in the press.

Instead of being sent to Fort Monmouth, as I expected, I was sent to Fort Dix for basic training along with a hundred or so draftees from New York City.

CHAPTER 2

JOINING THE ARMY

The cadre at Fort Dix was composed of regular army men. My top sergeant had a particular distaste for anyone except career soldiers. He was alerted to my arrival by the articles in the press. He saw to it that in addition to the drilling and marching and other duties related to basic training, I also had more than my share of kitchen police, garbage detail, latrine orderly duty, fireman and guard duty. I rarely met his exacting standard when it came to making up my bunk so he retaliated by "gigging" all 120 men in my barracks, depriving them of weekend passes. After a period of tension, the other men came to my aid and instructed me in making my bunk so that the top blanket was as taut as a drum head. The supply sergeant took special pleasure in providing me with uniforms which didn't fit, including a vintage World War I overseas cap.

Eventually, on Sunday, November 29th, I got my first 24-hour pass and I arranged with my father to spend it at the White House. With only a dollar and a half in my pocket, I hitchhiked to Washington in the driving rain. My first ride was with a traveling salesman headed for Philadelphia. He said he welcomed the opportunity to have someone to talk to. Then he began a tirade against President Roosevelt so vitriolic in tone that he seemed almost maniacal. He turned red as he spoke and gestured wildly. I couldn't interrupt him. Finally, I could stand it no longer. I got his attention by grabbing his arm and shaking him. I told him I had to get out—immediately. He stopped the car and I got out. As he drove off, I could hear him muttering and swearing to himself.

It was still pouring with rain. I seemed to be in the middle of nowhere. An hour passed before I got another ride. This one took me all the way to Washington and I was dropped off in front of the White House.

As soon as he greeted me, my father ordered me to get out of my wet uniform and into a hot tub. While I soaked there, he turned my uniform over to Arthur Prettyman, the president's valet, who ironed it dry. Wearing my father's dressing gown, I recounted my experiences in the army so far.

Dad looked thin and drawn. He seemed to be terribly ill but he assured me he was all right. He said he was having difficulty assimilating nourishment from his food and had to give himself injections every day. He demonstrated this by giving himself an injection in his thigh.

He told me that we would be having cocktails and supper with the president that evening. He said that Mrs. Roosevelt was away on a trip.

The president greeted me cordially in the Oval Study just down the hall from the Lincoln Bedroom that served as my father's quarters and office. With the president was his secretary, Missy LeHand. My father and I completed the group. As the president mixed up a shaker of dry martinis and served them to us, he asked me about army life. I told him much the same story I had recounted to my father, omitting, however, the unpleasant experience I had with the anti-Roosevelt fanatic who had given me a lift.

During supper, the president regaled us with stories which he told with great gusto. He said that during the afternoon he received a visit from the Secretary of the Treasury, Henry Morganthau, Jr. who expressed concern about the safety of the president in view of the war in Europe. Because the treasury secretary was responsible for the protection of the president, he proposed installing anti-aircraft batteries on the roof of the White House. The president rejected the idea immediately, saying he had no intention of transforming the White House into an armed camp. He told Secretary Morganthau that if he wanted to protect the president, he could put the anti-aircraft guns on the roof of the Treasury, next to the White House compound.

The president told one story after another and there was much laughter in that relaxed environment. The three of them—the president, my father, and Missy LeHand—worked together on matters of critical national importance every day. They were close friends and understood one another.

Suddenly, I realized it was past midnight and I had to get back to Fort Dix before reveille. I knew I couldn't reach the fort in time if I hitchhiked at that hour, so I asked my father if he would lend me five dollars so I could take a bus back. He said he didn't have it. Then the president said, "I'll lend you five dollars." I said I couldn't possibly take it from him, but he insisted. Then, taking a card bearing the presidential seal embossed in gold from the table next to him, he said, "Let me give you this in case you don't arrive in time for reveille." On it he wrote:

November 30, 1941

TO WHOM IT MAY CONCERN:

Private Robert Hopkins is to be excused from reveille. He has been in consultation with the Commander-in-Chief.

Franklin D. Roosevelt

Overwhelmed, I stammered my thanks.

Before leaving, I promised to repay the president the next day, right after I got paid. Then, concerned about my father's health, I asked him when he and my father would be taking a vacation.

"We'll go on vacation as soon as the aircraft strike is settled in California and the Japanese situation is resolved."

I knew about the strike at the aircraft factories, but I was unaware of any Japanese problem.

A week later, the Japanese attacked Pearl Harbor.

I was transferred to Ft. Monmouth and assigned to the Signal Corps Training Film Production Corps (TFPC). As I had been told, there were many Hollywood personalities there including Garson Kanin, Elia Kazan, William Holden, George Stevens, Carl Laemmle, Jr., and Arthur Laurents. They, and other experienced technicians whose names were unfamiliar to me, trained me in various aspects of filmmaking. I started out as a cutter, then went on as a film editor, a screen writer and assistant cameraman, working with a huge studio Mitchell camera. I began making training films working in various capacities.

Meanwhile basic training continued at Fort Monmouth. There were no rifles to be had, so we trained with broomsticks which had two nails partially pounded in to serve as sights. A soldier with a pencil was assigned to stand next to a target and mark it when we thought we had the bull's eye in our sights and called out "mark!" Cardboard cutouts labelled "tank" and other military equipment simulated targets for us.

I was able to get away to the White House again for a weekend. Mrs. Roosevelt invited Dad and me to a small dinner she was having in the Blue Room. She also invited Hollywood producer Walter Wanger and his beautiful raven-haired actress wife, Joan Bennett. The president was unable to attend.

Walter Wanger had just joined the Signal Corps film production unit at Ft. Monmouth as a major. He arrived resplendent in a dazzling white dress uniform with gold buttons. His wife, who I had seen in so many films, took my breath away. She seemed concerned about me. I think she thought I was too young to be in the army.

We sat down for dinner at a round table with Dad on Mrs. Roosevelt's right and I on her left. The major was next to me with his wife between him and my father. Major Wanger was particularly interested in talking to me about the unit to which we were both assigned and I told him all that I could.

As we talked, the butler began serving the first course, green pea soup. He was about to serve it to Major Wanger when his wife impetuously reached across him and patted me sympathetically on the thigh. This joggled the butler's hand and the hot soup poured on the major's lap.

There was considerable consternation by all. Mrs. Roosevelt dipped her napkin in her water glass and began dabbing at the spreading green stain, then thought better of it and asked the butler to take over. The major, who must have been in considerable pain, kept protesting that it was all right and nothing to be concerned about.

Mrs. Roosevelt ordered an usher to bring down one of the president's bathrobes and Major Wanger retired to the Green Room where he took off his trousers and put on the robe. The usher took away the trousers and somehow sponged them clean and pressed them dry.

I no longer remember what happened next, but I am sure the incident made an indelible impression on Major Wanger and his spouse—and that it was the topic of a lively discussion as they left the White House.

Encouraged by my father, I signed up for Officers Training School. The training consisted of climbing telephone poles, mastering the Morse code, learning how to splice wires, and learning the responsibilities of being a mess officer. I felt that I was moving farther and farther away from the film work I hoped to pursue in the army.

There we also closely followed the astonishing speed with which the Nazi Panzer divisions were advancing into Russia. Every day, the newspapers carried reports that hundreds and sometimes thousands of Russian towns and villages had fallen to the Germans in the previous twenty-four hours.

In the Spring of 1942 I received an invitation to the White House to attend my father's wedding to his third wife, Louise Macy, on July 30th. My father had introduced her to me previously at a rally in Madison Square Garden, where he was to give a speech. I had no idea then that they were romantically involved.

I managed to get permission from the army to attend the event, which was held at noon in the Oval Study on the second floor of the White House.

My older brother David was there with his wife Cherry, as were my younger brother Stephen and my half-sister Diana and some of Louise's family. Mrs. Roosevelt, of course, was present as well. The president served as best man. After the ceremony, the Marine string ensemble in the next room played "I Married an Angel" from a current Broadway show of that name. I had an opportunity to visit with president and Mrs. Roosevelt and with my family members during the buffet luncheon.

Before leaving I talked privately with my father and told him I was impatient to get overseas where all the action was. I told him my studies seemed to be leading me to become an officer in communications or worse yet a mess officer. He argued that I would be more comfortable in the army as an officer instead of as an enlisted man. I replied that it was more important to me to cover the war as an enlisted cameraman than to be an officer assigned to a rear area. He said the decision was mine.

I returned to Fort Monmouth that evening and resigned from the Officer Training School the next morning.

Shortly after I returned to TFPL it moved out of Ft. Monmouth to the long-abandoned Paramount film studios in Astoria, Long Island. There with better facilities we produced films which were much more professional.

But I was still eager to get overseas. When a combat training program was offered, I immediately signed up.

Knowing that I would soon be leaving for overseas, I invited my mother to the Stork Club for dinner. Leonard Lyons, a columnist at

Wedding of Harry Hopkins and Louise Macy at the White House on July 30, 1942.

the *New York Post*, had introduced me to the Stork Club when I worked for *The March of Time* and had expressed interest in seeing something of the nightlife in New York City. I visited him there frequently as he gathered material for his daily column. The regulars there were actors of the stage and screen as well as other entertainers. They included Orson Welles, Burgess Meredith, Paulette Goddard, Peter Arno, Abe Burrows, and Irving Berlin. They used the Cub Room as a kind of private club.

The night I took my mother there, Irving Berlin was sitting alone at the table across from us. When she was a young woman, my mother had been the private secretary to Katherine Mackay, whose daughter, Ellin, had married Irving. Mother was thrilled to meet him and told him that she used to help care for Ellin when she was a little girl. Irving was interested to learn about his wife's childhood. In course of their conversation, my mother told him she was working for the Red Cross and arranged entertainment for wounded soldiers at veterans' hospitals. She asked if he would be willing to visit the hospitals to raise the morale of the patients there. He agreed without hesitation.

On September 25, 1942, with all my training completed, I shipped out for England on a Dutch ocean liner called the *Dempo* which had been converted to a troop ship. We were part of a large

Irving Berlin, Ethel G. Hopkins and Robert Hopkins at the Stork Club in September 1942.

convoy escorted by swift destroyers, but we could travel only as fast as the slowest ship. The *Dempo* was so crowded with troops that the only space for us was outside on the top deck.

We took the North Atlantic route. These waters were infested with German U-boats. We were ordered not to smoke at night because the submarines allegedly could see the glow of our cigarettes. It was freezing cold as we skirted Greenland and Iceland. The ship's lines and rails were coated with ice. We slept on deck bundled up in our overcoats and wrapped in blankets. We were awakened at five o'clock in the morning when the ship's crew hosed down the decks.

Some of us managed to find refuge from the freezing water by scrambling on top of lockers containing life jackets. The rest could only stand on tip-toe to avoid being drenched.

The ocean swells were as high as the superstructure of the ship. The *Dempo* would plow into them and struggle to the top and teeter there. The ship shuddered when the propeller came out of the water, then would swoop down on the other side of the swell, only to face another just as large.

By this time I was a corporal and had been put in charge of the 70 men on deck with me. To keep warm and limber, I would lead them in calisthenics, one of which was jumping jacks. But with these enormous swells, when we jumped up, the deck followed us up or, alternately, it dropped away and we tumbled down, saved from rolling over the side only by the ship's railing.

Then one night we were awakened by a new motion of the ship which wallowed helplessly in the rough sea. The engine was silent. I learned that there was damage to the rudder. When we looked around us, the comforting presence of the convoy was nowhere to be seen. We were alone for a night and a day, a prime target for enemy submarines and the wild sea while the damage was being repaired. When we were again underway, and were no longer hampered by the slow ships of the convoy, we sped ahead at full speed, reaching Liverpool at about the same time as the convoy on October 9th.

CHAPTER 3

A WEEKEND WITH
PRIME MINISTER CHURCHILL

By October 15, 1942, I was in southern England where I had been assigned to Litchfield Barracks, a British army camp made partially available to U.S. troops. Two days later, I got a 24-hour pass and went to London. My first stop was the American embassy, where I checked in with Ambassador John G. Winant. He was pleased to see me because my father had been trying to locate me in England and had sent a cable to Prime Minister Churchill to this effect. The ambassador said he would send my father a message with my address.

I spent two interesting hours with the ambassador. He was a tall, soft-spoken man, with a shock of black hair that fell across his forehead. He was an admirer of Abraham Lincoln and there was something about him that reminded me of pictures of Lincoln. As he talked, he paced back and forth from one end to the other of the large room that was his office. When he walked away from me, his voice was so soft I could barely hear him. He excused himself to go to a meeting, but first he put me up in his apartment for the night. I had to return to Litchfield Barracks the following morning, so I saw very little of London on this visit.

Two days later, I received the following letter from 10 Downing Street bearing the seal of the prime minister:

10 Downing Street
Whitehall

17 October 1942

Dear Mr. Hopkins,

Your father, a great friend of all of us here, told Mr. Churchill that you were with the U.S. Army in England and I have just discovered (I hope correctly) how to address to you.

Mr. Churchill would very much like to make your acquaintance so will you please let me know when you are likely to be in London or could come up to meet him. I look forward to meeting you myself very soon.

Yours sincerely,
CR Thompson

P.S. By way of explanation I should add that I am a Personal Assistant to Mr. Churchill and know your father well. My address as there are two other Thompsons here is Commander C.R. Thompson.

I called Commander Thompson at 10 Downing Street and he told me that the prime minister was eager to meet me. He asked me when I could get down to London. I explained to him that I was only corporal in the army and was not free to travel at will. He told me not to worry about it, that I would hear more about this shortly.

I received orders to report to the American embassy on October 22nd for three days temporary duty. I arrived at the embassy that afternoon and was instructed by the officer on duty to report to Averell Harriman at the embassy in the morning.

With the evening free, I contacted Hannan Swaffer, a newspaperman working for *The Evening Standard*. He had been recommended to me by Leonard Lyons, a good friend of mine who worked as a columnist for the *New York Post*. Swaffer, as he preferred to be called, was an old-world type with long white hair in disarray. He chain-smoked and never took his cigarette from his mouth until he lit another one from it. It waggled up and down as he spoke, dropping ashes over his flowing bow tie and his vest.

He took me to a meeting of the Labor Party at which the archbishop of Canterbury, Dr. Temple, was to speak. Before the meeting, Swaffer introduced me to the archbishop and told him that I would soon be meeting with the prime minister. In his speech, the archbishop championed the idea of nationalizing British banks.

I met Averell Harriman at the embassy as arranged. He told me that the prime minister had invited me to accompany him on an inspection of the defenses of Dover.

We went to the railway station where the prime minister's private train was waiting. Winston Churchill was on the platform with a group of men when we arrived. He looked so exactly as I imagined him that I felt as if I had always known him. He greeted me warmly and introduced me to a distinguished-looking officer with a neat white beard, Field-Marshal Jan Smuts, prime minister of South Africa, and to his son. He also introduced me to Secretary Henry Morganthau, Jr., who had just arrived in England; to Sir Sidney Wood, the Chancellor of the Exchequer; to Major General Sir Hastings Ismay, who he addressed as "Pug"; to his son, Randolph Churchill, a British army captain; and to Commander "Tommy" Thompson, his personal aide, who had first contacted me.

The prime minister's train was fitted out with sitting rooms, bedrooms with private baths, and a comfortable dining room. The prime minister invited Averell, Randolph and me to join him for breakfast. He asked me about my Atlantic crossing and listened intently as I described that tempestuous voyage. When he asked what I had been doing since arriving in London, I described my meeting with the archbishop of Canterbury and quoted his remarks about nationalizing British banks. The prime minister's face darkened. He said, "The primate of England is a spiritual leader. He has no business meddling in politics."

Dover Castle is an ancient fortress, high on the white cliffs overlooking the English Channel. Across the water is the shore of France, twenty miles away. Secretary Morganthau handed me his 16-mm camera and asked if I would film this visit for him. So my first filming assignment in Britain was to cover Prime Minister Churchill's inspection of the defenses of Dover.

An honor guard greeted the prime minister and his guests in the cobblestone courtyard of the castle. Their precision drill and the clash of arms and the crash of their hobnailed boots on the cobblestones were impressive. We descended into the caverns underneath the castle, a honeycomb of passages and rooms carved out of the chalky cliffs. They contained a headquarters, a hospital, supply rooms, and a fire control station for the coastal cannons above ground. A mystical light illuminated the caverns from openings in the face of the cliff.

Back on the surface, we examined the enormous guns mounted on railway cars used to fire on targets on the French coast. Randolph urged his father to have the guns fire a few rounds on the Germans on the other side of the Channel. The prime minister refused his son's request, saying that no strategic or tactical purpose would be served and the Germans would just fire back on Dover, possibly killing civilians there.

On the way back to London, the prime minister invited me to Chequers for the weekend. I must admit I didn't know what "Chequers" was, but of course I accepted. He told Averell to take care of me until then.

Back in London, Averell invited me to stay overnight in his flat at the embassy. There I met Kathleen, his attractive daughter, and Pamela Churchill, Randolph's wife. Both were about my age. Kathleen worked for *Newsweek* as a reporter and had to dash off to cover Mrs. Roosevelt's arrival in London. Pamela and I went to the Washington Club—a Red Cross Club for soldiers—and had a Coca-Cola, my first since I left the States.

I had supper and spent the night at Averell's flat. I slept late and at about one o'clock had lunch with Kathie. Then she raced off again to catch up with Mrs. Roosevelt. Commander Thompson picked me up at three o'clock to take me to Chequers, which he described as the country residence of the prime minister. He encouraged me to call him "Tommy" as my father had done.

As we approached the estate, he told me that as a measure of security the original straight driveway to the house had been torn up and replaced by a different approach with a circle in front of the entrance to confuse the pilots of German bombers.

We were the first to arrive there so I had a fine opportunity to look around. Chequers is a tremendous English estate built in 1480. In about 1920, it was turned over to the incumbent prime minister to be used as a country home. Explicit instructions were given never to alter the place in any way–except of course to add amenities such as modern plumbing. The mansion for the most part has remained unchanged since sometime in the 16th century.

All the rooms have great high ceilings—the one in my bedroom must have been fifteen or twenty feet high—and in the downstairs Great Hall the ceiling was thirty-five feet high at least. It was an impressive room with a huge fireplace, heavy draperies, numerous pictures, armor, flags, spears, and comfortable furniture. Tommy told me that Rembrandt's painting *The Mathematician* had hung there, but was removed and placed in a vault for safekeeping until the end of the war.

Tommy took me to a small sitting room with a cozy fire, and introduced me to Mrs. Churchill, a handsome and charming woman, tall and aristocratic.

She served tea to us as she and I became acquainted. We were soon joined by Foreign Minister Anthony Eden and his wife. He was boyish-looking despite his moustache. I liked him immediately. His wife, I imagined, would be a hard person to know. She seemed completely overshadowed by him. Then Brendan Bracken arrived. Mrs. Churchill introduced him as the Minister of Information. He wore thick-lens spectacles and had an unruly shock of red hair. He greeted me warmly.

Just before dinner, Sir Arthur Harris, chief of Bomber Command, arrived with his young and extremely attractive wife, who was several years younger than he. The last addition to the group was Ambassador Winant.

Everyone remembered my father fondly, recalling his six-week stay in England during the Blitz in January 1941 when he came as President Roosevelt's emissary to Churchill to assess England's determination and needs to repel a German invasion which then seemed inevitable. It was his assessment that led to the massive Lend-Lease aid to England, a program that he administered.

After tea, everyone retired and dressed for dinner—that is, all except me. The women reappeared in long gowns, while Foreign Minister Eden and Air Chief Marshal Harris appeared in red and blue velvet dinner jackets, respectively. I felt rather out of place in my drab uniform. The prime minister wore one of the zipper "blitz" suits he invented and made famous. It was practical because it could be donned quickly in the event of a nighttime air raid. It looked rather like a pair of wooly coveralls.

We had an excellent dinner— partridge, I think. Also champagne, port and brandy. The prime minister assured me that all the food was grown on the grounds of the estate and that he complied with all the rules of rationing to which the English population was bound.

I noticed that after dinner they observed the old custom of letting the ladies retire first while the gentlemen remained to drink a glass of brandy and smoke cigars.

The prime minister insisted that I smoke a cigar. I demurred saying that while I smoked cigarettes and had smoked a pipe from time to time, I never smoked cigars. He persisted, saying that if I smoked a pipe, I could smoke a cigar. He gave me one of his huge Havana cigars and showed me how to pierce the end and roll the cigar between thumb and fingers to smell the aroma, then how to light it by letting the sulphur on the match burn away before touching the flame to the cigar. He warned me not to inhale.

The conversation centered around the successful British bombing of Genoa, which "Bomber" Harris described with considerable relish, revealing a blood-thirsty side to his character. The raid apparently was completely successful and all planes returned safely.

The first puffs of the cigar were agreeable, but the habit to inhale was hard to avoid and soon I began to feel ill. My forehead broke out in a sweat and I began to feel dizzy. I excused myself and found a bathroom where I lost that delicious dinner. I stubbed out the cigar and saved it for another time, then returned to the party feeling much better.

When we rejoined the ladies, the prime minister said that he had two films and that he would leave it to "our young American friend" to select which one to show. They were "The Lou Gehrig Story" and "All That Money Can Buy," an adaptation of Stephen Vincent Benet's short story "The Devil and Daniel Webster." Faced with the prospect of having to explain to a British audience the complexities of American baseball, I chose "All That Money Can Buy," recommending it highly to the prime minister. I had forgotten that in the jury selection scene, the devil had packed the jury box with the world's worst scoundrels, including Benedict Arnold. When the film was over, the prime minister turned to me and growled, "Well, of course, we have quite a different view of Benedict Arnold."

Ambassador Winant eased my embarrassment by relating the following story:

> An Englishman who was going to America encountered an American in a pub who, on learning of the Englishman's trip to his country, described it in most glowing terms. Touched by this, the Englishman said, "You must love your country very dearly—may I carry a message to anyone there for you?"
>
> The American fell silent, then sadly said, "No. No one there wants to hear from me. You see, my name is Benedict Arnold."

After the movie, the prime minister got the latest communiqués on the war. Among the prime minister's dispatches was one from my father which read:

Most secret for the prime minister. Your wire received. Give my love to Robert. Best of luck to your army in Libya.

The prime minister placed a call to my father at the White House using his scrambler telephone. He told my father of the result of the raid on Genoa, then turned the phone over to me so that I could speak to him for the first time since I left the States.

The prime minister had disappeared after I finished my call and I, assuming the party was over, said goodnight to the other guests and to Mrs. Churchill and went to bed.

The following morning, Sunday, I woke up at about nine o'clock. Except for Tommy Thompson, none of the others were up until 11:30. Miss Lemmon, the housekeeper, showed me through the public rooms of the historic house. It was not as large as I first imagined, but gave the illusion of grandeur.

When the prime minister came down to breakfast at 11:30, he scolded me roundly for leaving the party so early. He had simply left the room to deal with some dispatches. He said the party actually broke up at three o'clock in the morning. This, I learned, was the prime minister's daily routine.

Mary Churchill, the prime minister's pretty 20-year-old daughter, arrived at about noon. She was an officer candidate in the British Army Transport Service (ATS). Soon afterwards, Air Marshal Sir Charles Portal arrived with his wife. Then Mrs. Roosevelt came with her son, Elliott, a Lieutenant Colonel in the Eighth Air Force, whom I had not seen for some time. I had an opportunity to talk with Mrs. Roosevelt for a only short time before we all went in to dinner and she left almost immediately afterwards to visit a hospital for refugee children. I did, however, have a chance to talk to Elliott, since both he and I were invited back to Averell Harriman's apartment for supper that evening.

Before we left Chequers, Mary took Anthony Eden, Sir Charles Portal, Ambassador Winant, Elliott and me on a walk through the surrounding countryside—in the rain—to some Druid ruins on the top of a hill. We warmed ourselves in front of the fire in the great room before we took our leave. I thanked the prime minister and Mrs. Churchill for their warm welcome to me and the extraordinary visit I had with them.

CHAPTER 4

THE NORTH AFRICAN CAMPAIGN

lliott drove me back to Averell Harriman's apartment, where we had both been invited for supper. There, Averell introduced me to Darryl F. Zanuck, another supper guest, who was on leave from his position as president of Twentieth Century Fox Films. He was in the uniform of a full colonel in the Signal Corps. As we talked, my attention kept straying to his insignia of rank— silver eagles with diamond eyes. Colonel Zanuck told me that a "big show" was coming up and that I would be a part of it. He said he would be my commanding officer.

Back at Litchfield Barracks the following morning, on the 29th of October, I and others with me were ordered to Edinburgh by train and sent aboard the British cruise ship *Stratheden*, which had been converted to a troop carrier. There were thousands of American troops on board headed for a destination unknown to us. We were part of a huge convoy headed south.

For this voyage, I was billeted with 60 others on "H" deck, well below the waterline, in a cargo hold. I had the disturbing realization that if we were hit by a torpedo, this is where it would blast through the hull. The only ventilation came from blowers in the ceiling. We slept on hammocks strung above long tables where we ate. At night, with the motion of the ship, we swayed in our hammocks in unison. Some of my companions were seasick and the air was stale and smelly.

I succeeded in getting on the garbage detail, which involved dumping the food garbage off the stern of the ship at night so we would not be detected by enemy vessels. Here on deck the air was fresh and the sea was alight with phosphorous. As we moved farther south, it became exceedingly hot in the hold and I stayed out on deck as much as I could. During the day, dolphins played alongside the ship. We zig-zagged a lot to avoid German submarines. At one point, it was rumored we were only 200 miles from the coast of Florida.

One day, there was an exercise to test the guns and depth charges aboard the ship. I filmed it with my newly-issued 16-mm Filmo camera. Because it was so hot, I took off my jacket and hung it on an upright post. They fired a five-inch cannon off the stern of the ship. I was ready to film it and sat on a hatch cover from a position well in back of the gun. I was knocked on my back by the force of the blast and learned firsthand that the blast goes backward as well as forward. At one point in the exercise, all the 50-mm anti-aircraft guns, rockets and depth-charges seemed to be going off at once. I filmed it all. When it was over, I went back to retrieve my jacket, only to discover it was gone. When I told a sailor where I had left it, he told me I had hung it on an anti-aircraft rocket which was fired during the exercise.

Each morning I would get up early and go out on deck to stretch and look at the other ships in the convoy. But one morning, after we had been at sea for nine days, I was astonished to see that the ship was docked in port in a very busy city. Streetcars were going by a block away. There were Arab shoeshine boys at the foot of the gangplank as we debarked laden with equipment. It was November 8, 1942 and the North African landings were under way in Algiers.

Not a shot was fired. If not for our uniforms and equipment, we could have been tourists arriving that sunny morning at a tropical resort. Men in burnooses and heavily-veiled women watched us with some curiosity but no discernible hostility. This is not what I anticipated when Colonel Zanuck told me I would be taking part in a "big show."

A group of us were marched through the city to the Botanical Gardens, where we made camp, pitching our tents under exotic trees laden with heavily-perfumed blossoms. From there I could see that Algiers was built in a natural amphitheater. Pastel-colored houses covered the hills and swept down to the sparkling blue Mediterranean. The port was filled with ships of all descriptions.

On the second day, Colonel Zanuck ordered me to find a billet in town. I rented a small room costing the equivalent of two dollars a night on the Rue Michelet in the business section of the city. It was on the second floor. Its only window opened out onto an airshaft. Once installed, I reported to Colonel Zanuck at the Hotel St. Georges high on the hill overlooking the port. It had been established as Allied Force Headquarters under the command of Major

General Mark Clark. Colonel Zanuck introduced me to General Clark and informed him that I would serve as General Clark's liaison with the other photographers in the U.S. Army Pictorial Service while Colonel Zanuck was away filming the battles for a feature film he intended to produce. General Clark thoughtfully sent a cable to my father informing him of my safe arrival.

Enemy reaction to the invasion came on the following and succeeding days with repeated air raids on Algiers by German and Italian fighter-bombers. While we had plenty of anti-aircraft guns in the city and aboard ships in the harbor, we had no fighter aircraft to drive off the enemy in the air. I was glad that my room in the hotel was in the interior of the building and was therefore protected from the bomb blasts. I took care to leave the window open so that the glass would not be shattered by the concussion.

Colonel Zanuck drove alone to Casablanca, 700 miles away, concerned that the Twentieth Century Fox Film office there might have been damaged in the fighting. His office director was astonished to see him because the American troops had not yet taken the city. Satisfied that all was well, Colonel Zanuck returned to Algiers.

Before leaving for the front he instructed me to move into his room at the St. Georges Hotel and to prevent anyone else from usurping it. He ordered me to keep him supplied with film and boxes of his Havana cigars. He, in turn, would send me his exposed film so that I could send it to Washington for processing. Then he left, taking with him two motion picture cameramen, Sergeants Marshall "Sonny" Diskin and Earl Zeigler.

I gamely held onto Colonel Zanuck's room even though I was besieged by officers of increasingly high rank trying to take it from me. They argued that I was only a corporal and had no right to such quarters. I stood firm and said that I had explicit orders from a full colonel to hold onto this room for him. If they could come back with an officer of higher rank to supersede that order, then I would relinquish it. This did not occur.

As I received exposed film for processing from Colonel Zanuck, I sent him fresh film as well as a box of cigars disguised as film with each shipment so it would not be pilfered. As a further precaution, I dispatched these in a special red and white press pouch bearing the warning that it contained film and must not be opened.

Meanwhile, I carried out photographic and film assignments on war-related events in Algiers. General Clark instructed me to film the signing of the temporary armistice by Admiral Jean Darlan, the most senior Vichy French officer who, coincidently, was visiting his sick son at the time of our invasion.

The signing took place in a small room with very little light. I filmed it in black and white with my 35-mm Eyemo camera. I opened the aperture as wide as possible and prayed that my film was sensitive enough to record the event. It was not until 1993, at the commemoration of the 50th Anniversary of the Casablanca Conference in Morocco, that I saw an old newsreel film containing this footage showing that indeed there had been enough light to show the signing of this document which ended Vichy France's resistance in North Africa.

On another occasion, I was out on a routine assignment to take still pictures of a Signal Corps telephone exchange. On the way to the installation, my jeep was blocked by a pro-de Gaulle street demonstration. My driver could not find a way through the mob. I climbed out on the hood of the jeep with my camera in hand, and the crowd made way for us to get through. I went on to complete my assignment, then returned to headquarters.

Almost immediately, I received an urgent telephone call from Robert Murphy, who was a civilian advisor to General Clark. I hurried to his office and he asked me to find out which of the American army photographers was taking pictures of the Gaullist demonstration. He said the Gaullists were claiming that this represented official U.S. recognition of their cause. I told him that I was the photographer at the demonstration, but I took no pictures and used my camera simply as a way to get through the crowd. He told me that the U.S. position on General de Gaulle was ambivalent and that de Gaulle's followers in Algeria were hypersensitive about this. I promised him I would be careful in the future.

One morning, there was a tremendous explosion in the harbor during a German air raid. An ammunition ship had been hit by a bomb and caught fire. I grabbed my helmet, my 16-mm motion picture camera and several cassettes of color film, then dashed down to the port in my jeep. I ran out on the concrete jetty to a position where I had a clear view of the ammunition ship and began filming an effort by a U.S. destroyer to push the flaming ship out of the sea lane where it was blocking access to the docks.

At first there were no more explosions, but the fire had not been extinguished. With the prow of the destroyer against the stern of the ammunition ship, the destroyer began to move the ship slowly. Suddenly there was another huge explosion, the concussion of which knocked me to the ground while red-hot ragged fragments of steel whizzed over my

Document identifying Robert Hopkins as an Official War Photographer.

prone body and sizzled into the sea. The heat of the explosion was so intense that it welded the destroyer to the ammunition ship.

More explosions followed and I didn't dare stand up for fear of being hit by shrapnel. I fervently prayed to God asking that I be spared from this and other dangers of war. Although I didn't belong to any church, I prayed frequently and sometimes felt that God answered me. When He did not, I realized my entreaty was too frivolous. This time, however, His answer was unmistakable. He said I would survive this and the other rigors of war. My faith in His message led me into perilous situations in the months and years which followed.

Lying on my stomach, I continued to film the fiery scene in front of me until I had used all of my film. Then, crawling crablike, I made my way back to my jeep and drove back up to Allied Force Headquarters.

Later, when the fire was out and the ships had cooled down, the navy was able to tow both ships out of the harbor and clear of the sea lanes.

When Colonel Zanuck and his crew returned from the front, Diskin and Zeigler told me that when they were attacked by a German Stuka fighter plane, Zanuck tried to shoot it down with his Tommy gun. Unaccustomed to the recoil, Zanuck lost his balance and fell backwards onto a cactus. Diskin and Zeigler had the inglorious task of picking cactus spines out of his backside for an hour.

On December 4th, Colonel Zanuck told me he was going back to the United States to edit the film he and his crew had shot. He promised me that he would contact my mother and father and assure them that I was all right. He was as good as his word. Before leaving, he asked me to call him after the war. I said that I would, but didn't give it another thought.

I was eager to get up to the front, and asked General Clark if he could arrange it. He saw to it that I was attached to a small unit of army G-2 (intelligence) under Captain Marcel Simon, an American of French origin. My task was to photograph captured German military equipment.

We operated from several different towns, including Souk Arras, Souk el Araba and Souk el Kemis—towns all named for the day the market was held in each. Finally, we were installed in an abandoned house in the town of Medjez-el-Bab, where I set up my lab. The house was teaming with cockroaches which got into my photographic paper and munched on it. They apparently liked the taste of the emulsion.

German and Italian planes attacked the town repeatedly. The French inhabitants had evacuated, leaving only the Arab inhabitants. I photographed scores of German tanks, vehicles of all descriptions, artillery guns and other equipment. I also photographed and filmed German prisoners who didn't seem to be at all sorry to have been captured. They carried on in front of the camera like playful children.

Because there were so few official army photographers in this sector of North Africa, we were usually assigned to a division and were authorized to attach ourselves to any army unit that was in action. When that unit was relieved, we were to attach ourselves to another that was in contact with the enemy. This informal arrangement gave us more freedom of movement than that experienced by most soldiers. The downside was that we were almost always in action. While most army commanders were pleased to have us with them, they never really considered us to be a part of their contingent because we were not on their roster. As a result, we rarely were paid on time. The enlisted men liked to have us with them because if our films were shown in the newsreels, their families might see them and know that they were all right.

Mail delivery from home was irregular at best. I had been away from the United States for over two months before I received my first letter. It was from my father and it had been hand carried to me by Leon Henderson, who was on a mission to North Africa. The letter gave me news about my older brother, David, who was a lieutenant JG in the navy; and about my younger brother, Stephen, who was at Hill School in Pennsylvania. With it was a packet containing a wallet and $25, Dad's gift to me for Christmas.

I finished my G-2 assignment a week before Christmas and was put in command of a camera unit consisting of two still photographers, two motion picture cameramen and the driver of a two-and-a-half-ton truck which had been placed at our disposal. We were assigned to cover the advance of the 13th Armored Regiment.

The Germans and the Italians had full command of the air, so whenever we were on the road one of us would stand on the tailgate of the truck and fire his pistol if an aircraft was spotted. On hearing the shot, our driver would jam on the brakes and we would all dash as far away from the truck and the road as we could to avoid being strafed by the plane.

As I was filming the regiment's column of tanks passing a road sign showing how far we had advanced, I and my companions were confronted by a group of British soldiers with their guns pointed at us. They commandeered our weapons, our truck and camera equipment and marched us unceremoniously to a British army camp nearby. When we arrived, they locked us up in a makeshift but effective jail.

Once they had us under lock and key, they informed us that we were spies and that appropriate action would be taken by the authorities. I protested that we were official U.S. Army photographers with the specific assignment to record the war. They demanded documents to confirm this. We had never been issued any and could produce none. They accused us of photographing a secret British installation—and indeed—although I did not notice it at the time—the installation in which we found ourselves was in the background of the scene I was filming when we were accosted.

They left us alone with a guard outside our prison bars. We began to discuss our plight and my companions pointed out that the British execute spies and that I had better do something to get us out of this predicament.

I called the guard over and demanded to speak to the Officer of the Guard. In due time, he appeared. I told him that I could not help but feel that Prime Minister Churchill would be extremely irritated if he learned that this unit had imprisoned the son of his good friend, Harry L. Hopkins, Lend-Lease Administrator. I was able to produce the letter I had received from my father, written on White House letterhead, to prove my identity.

The officer left without comment, taking my letter with him. About 45 minutes later, he returned with my letter and released us.

He returned our truck, weapons and equipment and said goodbye. He did not apologize.

Later, when I was again at Allied Forces Headquarters in Algiers, I described this incident to General Clark and requested that he have a document issued to all combat cameramen, identifying them as official army photographers with authority to provide information to the War and Navy Departments in Washington and to the War Office in London for official pictorial war records. I said that it should be signed by an official of senior enough in rank to impress Allied field commanders.

On April 25, 1943, I received such a document bearing my photograph and serial number, identifying me as an official war photographer. It was written in English and in French and signed by Major General W.B. Smith, Chief of Staff, Allied Force Headquarters. It was accompanied by a cloth flash with the words "Official War Photographer" to be stitched to the sleeve of my uniform. Each army photographer received one, bringing to an end problems such as the one we encountered.

We caught up to the 13th Armored Regiment, which was bivouacked in an olive grove near Pont de Fas in Tunisia. An incessant, dismal rain fell all day long and we were in mud well above our ankles. My home was a half-track armored vehicle covered with a tarpaulin. I stayed there in an unsuccessful attempt to keep dry.

On Christmas Eve a few of us sang carols. When we finished, we heard Christmas carols being sung in German. Only then did we realize how close we were to the enemy. Obviously, there was a tacit truce that rainy Christmas Eve.

On Christmas day we were awakened by the beautiful sound of church bells in the clear morning air. Most of the men received the best present that any soldier in the field can get—mail from home! Mine was probably back at Allied Force Headquarters. Nevertheless, I was grateful to have received that one letter from my father which may have saved our lives.

I filmed the men receiving and reading their mail. Perhaps their families would see the film on the newsreels and know that their boys were alive and well. Everyone got a ration of cigarettes and I decided to smoke the cigar given to me by the prime minister.

Later, we moved out and concealed the armored vehicles under trees on a wooded knoll. Around noon, a Stuka flew directly over us and we sighed with relief because we thought the pilot had not seen us. But then, in a remarkable maneuver, he dropped his flaps and seemed to pivot in midair, dropping to an altitude of about 300 feet. He returned with his machine guns blazing and dropped a bomb close to our half-track. I was with two soldiers. One was killed outright and the other had his leg blown off. I was virtually untouched with only tiny scratches on my right calf. There were two or three drops of blood, which I wiped off. I certainly was not going to apply for a Purple Heart for such a superficial wound.

The dead soldier received last rites from the army chaplain, who gently removed the contents of his pockets, listing everything in a notebook along with the soldier's name, rank and serial number. He then cut off one of the dog tags, leaving the other around the soldier's neck. The chaplain tied the personal belongings in a handkerchief with the dog tag attached to the outside. Meanwhile, the medics attended to the soldier who had lost his leg.

This was the first time anyone close to me had been killed or wounded in the war. It was a sobering experience.

Nearly 30 years later, I noticed a small hard bump over my right eyebrow. I kept touching it for several weeks as it pushed further and further out, until I was able to remove it. There was no blood. It was about a 16th of an inch long and pointed on each end. Whatever it was seemed to be encased in a kind of cyst. I cut it open and there was a small, black, exceedingly hard object in the center. Curious, I brought a magnet close to it and the object immediately adhered to it. There was no doubt in my mind that this was a tiny fragment of shrapnel from that bomb blast. At intervals of six or seven years, two more fragments emerged in the same way from above my right eyebrow.

We moved again. I attached myself to the 1st Battalion while my companions covered the activities of the other units of the 13th Regiment. The 1st Battalion deployed its tanks and half-tracks to attack the German armored unit on the other side of a hill. I prepared to film the attack.

It was immediately evident when we attacked that the German force was much more powerful, better equipped and more skillful than we were. Our unit had Sherman tanks with steel plates riveted together. The Germans had swift, smooth-seamed welded Tiger tanks with 88-mm cannon. One would come out in the open, luring us from protective cover. Then another tank would fire on us. When they hit our tanks with 88-mm rounds, the rivets would sheer off, killing or maiming the tank crew. In no time, they disabled three of our tanks.

We withdrew to await nightfall.

We were supported by a French artillery outfit with 75-mm rifles mounted on flatbed trucks. Anticipating a German attack, our commander asked them to watch out for German tanks and knock them out as they rounded a curve in the road.

Late that night, we heard the grounding roar of approaching tanks. The French artillery was alert. As the tanks rounded the bend in the road, the French disabled them in rapid succession. When we examined them, we were dismayed to realize they had knocked out our own tanks. The bodies of those killed were removed and the survivors were treated. The damaged tanks were loaded onto tank recovery units.

Our commander told us to prepare to withdraw sometime during the night. I stretched out my canvas shelter-half on the muddy ground after asking the commanders of the tanks on either side of me to wake me before pulling out. Then I wrapped myself in a blanket and went sound asleep, sinking into the soft mud.

At dawn the following morning, I was shocked to see that the entire battalion of tanks and other vehicles had moved out and were nowhere in sight. It was a miracle that I was not squashed by one of them. Since I was not a regular member of the battalion, they had simply forgotten to wake me.

There was no one about. Obviously, I was behind German lines and there was no way of knowing which way to walk toward friendly forces. The ground had frozen during the night and I had to rip my shelter-half from the frozen earth, leaving the imprint of my body in the ground.

I had no food except the hard chocolate bar to be used as emergency rations. We were told in training that with a knife, the chocolate could be shaved into water and made into a hot or cold chocolate drink, or it could be bitten off and eaten. We were assured that it would keep us alive for several days.

I tried shaving it into my cup with water from my canteen, but it would not dissolve. I didn't want to light a fire because of the proximity of the Germans. I drank it cold, but it was awful. Later, I tried to bite off a piece, but it was too hard.

I occupied myself by tentatively exploring the area. I could hear the voices of the Germans, but I couldn't see them. Then I saw a slight movement on the side of a nearby hill. I looked carefully and realized it was an Arab armed with a long antique-looking rifle. His burnoose was the color of the earth, making him almost invisible. As I looked around, I saw several more—eight in all. They were *Goums*,

Moroccans fighting for the French. One of them spotted me and signalled me to approach.

Fortunately, they spoke French. I described my situation and asked them if they had any food. They produced a marvelous hot meal of spaghetti with a delicious sauce, which I devoured hungrily. Then I asked them if they could direct me to American lines. They said that they could, but they would have to finish their mission first.

I stayed with them for three days and nights. Their mission was to terrorize the Germans. They accomplished this by silently creeping up on German sentries at night and slitting their throats. Then they moved into the German camp and killed sleeping soldiers and officers. They never used their guns. By the end of the third day, the remaining Germans moved out and the *Goums* directed me toward American lines the next morning.

They were courageous and effective soldiers. I owe my life to them.

I arrived at a replacement depot on New Year's Eve. This was a center where soldiers who had been separated from their own units for one reason or another were reassigned to their own or other units, usually the infantry. They were a pretty rough bunch. They had found liquor somewhere and several of them were roaring drunk.

I was concerned that my family might have been informed that I was missing in action. I needn't have worried. Apparently no one bothered to mention the fact that I was not where I was supposed to be. This, of course, was another drawback to the informal manner in which we attached ourselves to whatever unit was in contact with the enemy, then detached ourselves when they were drawn out of action.

We were billeted in the ruins of a farmhouse. All of the windows and doors had been blown out and the roof had been demolished, so it was almost like being out of doors. After I registered and got something to eat, I wrapped my cameras and film in my raincoat, using it as a pillow. I put my Colt .45 revolver under it, to be used in case things got out of hand.

I managed to get to sleep only to be awakened by the crowing of a rooster. The man next to me groaned, rolled over and picked up his rifle. He fired through the window without getting up, killed the rooster with a single shot, then went back to sleep.

At the replacement depot, I learned that elements of the 13th Armored Regiment were in the vicinity of Bizerte, on the coast of the Mediterranean. I managed to get a lift on a supply truck, but learned from a British quartermaster outfit bivouacked on the outskirts of the town that the regiment had moved out.

Bizerte had been severely bombed and the port facilities destroyed. The biggest building still standing was a vacant hotel. I took shelter there in a room with a bed on the third floor. After settling in, I filmed and photographed the extensive destruction to the port facilities and the town itself. Cranes used to load and unload ships had been demolished, reduced to twisted heaps of metal. Huge chunks of concrete had been blasted from the pier, preventing ships from coming alongside. The town was without fresh water and there was no electricity. Most of the local inhabitants had moved out.

I encountered a hundred or more English solders waiting in line single file in the center of town. On investigation, I learned that the British army, as was its practice, had taken over the local brothel. Here, for a few shillings, the soldiers could relieve their sexual frustrations.

I returned to the hotel for a rest. It was hot and I stripped down to my undershorts and fell asleep.

I was awakened by an air raid alert. I grabbed my helmet, put on my shoes and shirt, then laden down with my cameras, my film and my pistol, I raced down the stairs and ran as far as I could away from the hotel, collapsing breathless in a ditch as the roar of planes came closer. The German planes seemed to focus their attention on the hotel, perhaps because it was still standing. I tried to film the raid, but the light was fading that evening and I had little hope that the pictures would come out. When the dust had settled, the hotel was in ruins. I couldn't even see where my room had been. I vainly searched for my raincoat, my blanket and other parts of my kit, but they were buried under the rubble. Fortunately, I had my helmet, my camera equipment and my film. But there I was, without trousers, a jacket or even socks.

The British quartermasters came to my aid. They fitted me out with British-issue trousers, two pairs of socks, two handkerchiefs and a British battle-jacket. They put me up in their encampment for the night.

The next morning, I filmed the effects of the bombing. Finding a shop undamaged and open, I bought a loaf of bread, some cheese and a bottle of red wine for lunch. I tucked the bottle of wine inside my battle-jacket. On the way back, I met a French woman and her teenage daughter who were standing on the steps of their home, which was undamaged. I stopped and we talked about the bombing the previous night. They seemed relieved that I spoke French and were interested that I was an American.

As we chatted, a British soldier, obviously very drunk, approached. Seeing the attractive young girl, he made it very clear, even though he didn't speak French, that he wanted to have sex with her. Obviously, he was fed up with the endless waiting in the brothel line. The mother appealed to me for help. The soldier, realizing that I spoke the language, asked me to tell her what he wanted. I urged him to go home and leave them alone, but he would hear none of this. He became belligerent. To pacify him, I told him I would talk to them. Reverting to French, I explained the situation and told them that at my signal, they must immediately go back into the house and lock and bar the door, which they did.

When he saw what happened, the soldier accused me of not translating what he said. I told him to go back to his camp and sleep it off. He took offense at this, and with a stream of obscenities began fingering his rifle. I waved him goodbye, turned my back on him and walked away. His inexhaustible vocabulary of invective continued and I heard him draw back the bolt on his rifle. Without looking back, I knew it was loaded and aimed at me. I kept walking at the same pace, but my heart was pounding. I fancied I could feel the place in my spine where his bullet would find me.

Then, the unexpected happened. The bottle of red wine slipped out from under my battle jacket and fell to the ground, breaking in half.

There was a moan of distress from the soldier. I looked around and saw that he had lowered his rifle and had his eyes riveted on the bottom half of the bottle, which was still standing upright, filled with wine.

"If you want it, it's yours," I told him.

His animosity melted away. I walked on and he scooped up the bottle and made off with it.

Never before or since, have I felt so close to death.

I was eager to get back to my camera unit, which I assumed was still attached to the 13th Armored Regiment, the remnants of which had probably moved up toward Tunis. I hitched a ride in that direction and was told by the driver that the battle was reaching its climax and that Germans and Italians were surrendering in droves.

I located my unit and we shared our adventures since I last saw them. They told me our driver had vanished and no one knew what became of him. They said the British were rapidly advancing on Tripoli. It was evident that when Tunis and Tripoli were captured, the war in North Africa would be over. After I sent my exposed film back to our headquarters in Algiers, we spread out to cover what we thought were the last stages of the North African campaign.

The rain had started again and the movement of trucks and armored vehicles transformed the roads into bogs of mud. Abandoned German and Italian equipment was everywhere and long lines of the enemy waited to be disarmed and processed as prisoners of war. The fighting was still going on in Tunisia, but the rain and mud hindered operations. We had our hands full in the days that followed covering the climax of the campaign.

Then, one morning, a U.S. Army colonel approached me.

"Are you Corporal Robert Hopkins?" he asked.

"Yes, sir."

"What's your serial number?"

"32183182, Sir."

"You have orders to report back to Allied Force Headquarters in Algiers."

"No, sir," I replied. "I'm here to cover the fall of Tunis."

"Son, you're a corporal and I'm a colonel. I'm ordering you to go back to Algiers RIGHT NOW!"

"Yes, sir! How am I supposed to get back there?"

"Hitchhike," he replied.

So, disappointed and puzzled at having to leave at this critical time, and without written orders, I said goodbye to the members of my unit and tried to find my way back to Algiers. It took me three days to get there. I first tried to fly, but the only U.S. planes in the vicinity were recently-arrived P-38 fighter planes which had no room for passengers. I got aboard a French plane, but we landed farther away from Algiers than I started. Finally, I got a ride on the back of a French truck along with some Arab workmen.

Bone-tired from the trip, I reported to General Clark at Allied Force Headquarters. It was at this meeting that I told him about our incarceration by the British.

"You're in the wrong city, corporal. You're supposed to be in Casablanca," he said. "I'll put you on General Bedell Smith's plane tomorrow morning. In the meantime, get cleaned up and take plenty of film with you." I asked him what my assignment was.

"You'll find out when you get there."

I showered and shaved, then stocked up on film for my cameras. At six o'clock the following morning, I met General Smith at the Maison Blanche airport, which had been taken over by our air force.

General Smith and I were the only passengers on the C-47 aircraft. We talked about the war and he asked what I did before I signed up for the army, but he didn't give me even a hint about my assignment in Casablanca.

CHAPTER 5

THE CASABLANCA CONFERENCE

In Casablanca, General Smith directed me to an office where I was to report. Encumbered by my cameras and equipment, I knocked on the door and entered when a voice said to come in. I saluted.

"Corporal Hopkins reporting as directed, sir."

"What the hell are you doing here, soldier? And where did you get that uniform?" he asked. I looked at the officer for the first time. Seated at his desk, on one side of which was his highly polished helmet, and the other side his ivory-handled Colt revolver, was General George Patton.

"Sir, I have no idea," I said with some confusion. "I'm a U.S. Army combat cameraman. I was in Tunisia preparing to film the capture of Tunis when I was ordered back here." I explained that I lost part of my uniform in a German bombing and the British had provided the missing elements.

"I want you in an American uniform," he barked. Then he pushed a button on his desk and ordered the captain who entered to take me to "Villa 2" and then see to it that I was issued a new uniform.

As we drove up through the city, I was surprised to see the extraordinary security measures which had been taken. There were barbed wire entanglements at various points with sentries patrolling in pairs accompanied by guard dogs. Planes circled above the city. We were stopped repeatedly at army checkpoints. Why, I wondered, was there all this security so far from enemy lines?

The command car pulled up in front of a villa labelled "Dar es Saada" near the Anfa Hotel. To one side was a sign reading "Villa 2." The captain told me that this was where I got out. I unloaded my equipment and headed up the path to the front door. There was a

Robert and his father Harry Hopkins at Casablanca on January 14, 1943.

civilian at the door who let me in. At the time, I thought he looked familiar, but I couldn't place him. Then I remembered he was a Secret Service agent I knew at the White House. Puzzled, I entered the living room.

To my astonishment, I was greeted by my father, who was as surprised as I. I assumed he was there on another mission for President Roosevelt. A roar of laughter drew my attention to the other side of the room. I turned and saw that it was President Roosevelt himself. The president in Morocco! It was hard to believe. Without telling my father, he had instructed General Eisenhower to find me and have me sent back from the front.

In response to my question, my father told me that he and the president had come to Casablanca to meet with Prime Minister Churchill. He said that Stalin had been invited, but couldn't come because of the bitter fighting in the Battle of Stalingrad. Then the president added that he wanted me to cover the conference for the White House. I was overwhelmed. My father disclaimed any responsibility for this. It was not in his nature to permit me or my brothers to enjoy any special privileges because of his position in the White

House, and I understood this. The president said I would be quartered with Mike Reilly and the rest of the Secret Service contingent in the Villa Dar es Saada, in a room just off the living room. The president invited me to sit down and have lunch with them.

"Tell me about the war," he said.

I described all that I had seen and experienced. My father was upset to learn that I had been taken prisoner, even if it was by the British, but the president was amused by the story. Dad was even more concerned when I told them I had been left behind German lines by the 1st Battalion of the 13th Armored Regiment. He said that I should be attached to a single unit and should stay with it where ever it was sent. I replied that there were so few official photographers that the filmed record of the war would be incomplete if we were anchored to a single unit.

After lunch, I went down into the city and was issued a new American uniform. When I returned, Dad told me to be prepared to take some pictures the following day, January 20th. He suggested I turn in early and get a good night's sleep. Then he received the following hand-written note from Tommy Thompson on behalf of the prime minister:

Tuesday

Dear Harry,

The P.M. would be very pleased if you would come & dine tonight and bring Robert with you. Would you also ask Elliott and Franklin Jr. if they can come?

The P.M. hopes that Randolph will have arrived & there will be a family party.

Yours, Tommy

When Dad and I arrived, we found Randolph with his father, Tommy Thompson, and General Sir Harold Alexander. Then President Roosevelt arrived with Elliott and Averell Harriman. Franklin Roosevelt, Jr. was on duty on a destroyer in the Mediterranean and did not arrive until the next day. Randolph had parachuted into Yugoslavia and was attached to Marshal Tito's staff. He had managed to get away in time to meet his father in Casablanca.

This was the first time I had seen the president, my father and Winston Churchill together. Their conversation was easy and ranged over the entire expanse of the war. General Alexander gave us a vivid description of the British 8th Army's campaign in Tripolitania. I was fascinated to listen to them talk. Randolph, however, kept interrupting. He obviously had been drinking and his remarks were of little importance. Finally, I told him to knock it off. Wounded, he said, "You're supposed to be on my side!" But he kept relatively quiet after that.

Prime Minister Churchill took us all inside his mobile map room, where he could watch the progress of the war on all fronts throughout the world. He was very proud of this and it obviously impressed President Roosevelt as well. Subsequently, the president established a Map Room in the White House, patterned on the one he saw that evening.

Dad had arranged for a quartet from a U.S. Army Negro unit that was attached to my unit to sing during dinner. They sang spirituals but weren't prepared to sing the Prime Minister's request for "You Are My Sunshine." Instead, they sang "Ezekiel Saw a Wheel." At the chorus, when they sang "Ain't Gonna Study War No More," the president nodded his head and said "Those are my sentiments too." Nevertheless, conversation about the progress of war was on everyone's mind.

After dinner, Churchill took me to one side and said, "I want you to take a picture of your father and me, walking along the beach deciding the fate of nations, with the mighty surf of the Atlantic crashing against the rugged, rocky shore." Churchill's eloquence was evident whenever he spoke. His rich vocabulary, his sense of drama, his understanding of history, and his experience as a journalist combined to give his words great force. I promised I would look for the proper location the next day and take the picture he requested.

The next morning I scouted the beaches around Casablanca, but all were sown with mines and covered with barbed wire entanglements. Furthermore, there was no rocky shore and the Atlantic waves rolled in smoothly over the broad sandy beaches. I reported to the prime minister that there simply was not the setting he had so vividly described. Years later, after the war, when I reviewed the photographs I had taken I kept looking for the one Churchill had engraved in my memory, a photo I never took.

The Combined British and American Chiefs of Staff had arrived several days prior to the arrival of President Roosevelt and Prime Minister Churchill. At the outset, it was the Combined

The Anfa Hotel, site of the Casablanca Conference.

American and British Chiefs of Staff who bore the burden of the deliberations. Their task was to assess the options proposed by the chiefs of state concerning Allied military action to be taken world-wide after our victory in North Africa.

While these talks were in progress, the president and the prime minister had time to deal with the thorny problem of French participation in the rest of the war. The problem was to determine who would lead Free French forces. Both General Charles de Gaulle and General Henri Giraud were invited to the Casablanca Conference to resolve this problem. The president hoped that a joint command could be arranged to avoid the impression that he and Churchill were imposing a single leader who might then aspire to become president of France, with Allied backing. General Giraud arrived promptly, but General de Gaulle, sensing that he might be asked to share this responsibility, demurred.

On the morning of January 20th, the Combined Chiefs of Staff reported the results of their deliberations to the president and the prime minister, who approved the strategies to be taken. I was then

The Combined British and American Chiefs of Staff when they agreed on the invasion of Sicily.

called in and photographed the Combined Allied Chiefs of Staff with the president, the prime minister and my father in the dining room of the president's villa. Those present were Lieutenant General H.H. (Hap) Arnold, Admiral Ernest J. King, General Sir Alan F. Brooke, Admiral of the Fleet Sir Dudley Pound, General George C. Marshall, Brigadier E.I.C. Jacob, Lieutenant General Sir Hastings Ismay, Vice Admiral Lord Louis Montbattan, Brigadier General John R. Deane, Field Marshal Sir John Dill and Air Chief Marshal Sir Charles Portal. Just 14 men combined to map out and approve strategies which would have an impact on the course of war around the world. I wonder how many it would take to make those judgments today.

That evening, I had dinner with President Roosevelt, my father, Averell Harriman, Elliott Roosevelt and Robert Murphy. Bob Murphy had been deeply involved in the negotiations concerning the role of the French in pursuit of the war after the North African campaign was over. He was the primary contact with General Giraud and reported directly to Generals Clark and Eisenhower. The conversation focused on the difficult negotiations between Generals Giraud and de Gaulle. But it was evident that de Gaulle's refusal to come to Casablanca to meet with Giraud in the presence of

Roosevelt and Churchill increasingly irritated the president. At that dinner and at most of the other informal lunches and dinners at which I was present, this topic dominated the conversation. The president jokingly referred to de Gaulle as a reluctant "groom" who would not show up at the altar for the wedding with the "bride" (Giraud). When he finally did show up, the president was quite curt with him.

After a series of meetings and prodding from Roosevelt and Churchill, de Gaulle and Giraud finally agreed to work together by forming a National Committee for the Liberation of France on which they would serve as co-chairmen, with General Giraud in command of Free French Armed Forces and de Gaulle responsible for political initiatives designed to unite the French people in the struggle against German occupation of France.

The next day, January 21st, President Roosevelt was scheduled to inspect elements of the American troops which had taken part in the invasion of North Africa, and then to go on to Port Lyautey, where some of the original landings had taken place.

General Patton lined up the troops in single file, shoulder-to-shoulder, facing the highway leading to Port Lyautey. It was a surprise inspection and the troops, standing at attention, had no idea who the inspecting officer would be. I filmed them as we drove by slowly and I was amused to see their jaws drop open when they realized it was the president of the United States inspecting them.

When we got beyond the troops, the president's convoy picked up speed. I rode in the command car with the Secret Service, directly behind the limousine in which the president rode. As we sped along at 60 miles an hour, a French civilian car behind us attempted to pass us, blowing its horn incessantly. The Secret Service men sprang into action, tommy guns in hand, but Mike Reilly ordered our driver to force the car behind us off the road into the desert as he attempted to pass. I have no way of knowing whether the driver of that car was simply curious to know who was in the convoy or if he had a more malevolent mission in mind.

At Port Lyautey we saw the ruins of the fort which had been destroyed in the fierce fighting between the American soldiers and the French army defenders under the command of the Vichy government. The president laid a wreath at the graveyard of the American soldiers killed in that conflict.

I photographed the president, my father, General Clark and General Patton having lunch in the field out of army mess kits.

During lunch, General Patton briefed them on the bitter battle fought there.

I think everyone was tired when we returned to Casablanca that evening. After captioning my pictures and film and dispatching them to the War Department, I turned in without supper and slept soundly until dawn.

The president asked me to take pictures the following evening at a dinner party to which he had invited the Sultan of Morocco and Prime Minister Churchill. The sultan was accompanied by his 13-year-old son, Crown Prince Moulay Hassan; the Grand Vizier, Haj Mohammed El-Mokri; the Director of Royal Protocol, Si Mohammed El Maammeri; and the Resident General from Vichy France, General Auguste Nogues. At the time, Morocco was a French protectorate and General Nogues held the key posts in the Moroccan government of minister of foreign affairs and minister of national defense. He seemed uneasy in the presence of Roosevelt and Churchill. Other guests were my father, General Patton, Bob Murphy, Elliott Roosevelt, and Roosevelt's naval aide Captain Eddy. The president introduced me to the sultan and his entourage. I then took pictures of the entire group. The crown prince showed a lively interest in my cameras, and I demonstrated how each of them worked. I then withdrew since I was not invited to the dinner itself.

I later learned from my father that during dinner President Roosevelt spoke in glowing terms about the post-war era when oppressed people of the world would be liberated. Dad said that Churchill scowled at this but remained silent while General Nogues, whose mission it was to keep Morocco firmly under the thumb of Vichy France, looked exceedingly uncomfortable.

A half-century later, some 70 former diplomats, historians and descendants of the participants in the Casablanca Conference celebrated the 50th anniversary of that event at the invitation of King Hassan II, the former crown prince. I was one of that group. In fact, of those in attendance, only the king and I participated in the original conference.

The king graciously received us at his palace in Fez. He revealed that after dinner, Roosevelt spoke privately with the sultan and told him he was confident that Morocco would regain its sovereignty from France within ten years. This prophecy was fulfilled when France relinquished Morocco as a protectorate in 1953. King Hassan II traced the beginning of the road to Morocco's independence from the dinner his father had with President Roosevelt in 1943.

Roosevelt and Churchill at Casablanca on January 24, 1943.

The king told us another interesting story. He said that despite the tight security at the time of the conference, Nazi agents learned that President Roosevelt was meeting with Prime Minister Churchill in Casablanca and cabled a message to Berlin to this effect. In deciphering the message, the German code clerk in Berlin translated "Casablanca" as "The White House," inadvertently leading the Nazi high command to believe that the meeting was being held in Washington. Had the message been delivered as written, the Nazis might well have shelled or bombed the meeting site, possibly killing Roosevelt and Churchill, as well as their senior military advisors, thus altering the course of the war.

On Sunday, January 24th, I had breakfast with Dad and Averell Harriman. We were now moving into the final phase of the Casablanca Conference. Dad told me there would be a press conference at noon and

Generals Giraud and de Gaulle at the Casablanca Conference with Roosevelt and Churchill on January 24, 1943.

that we would leave Casablanca immediately afterward and drive to Marrakech for a day's rest before the return home. He said that Roosevelt wanted me to cover the trip back to the United States as well.

This caught me by surprise. I said that much as I wanted to see my mother and brother, I wasn't ready to leave. I wanted to return to Tunisia and cover the remainder of the African campaign and then continue to film the next phase of the war, wherever that might be. I asked him if he would plead my case with the president. I think he was pleased with my decision because he was so completely involved in the war himself. He said he would do what he could.

De Gaulle and Giraud arrived at the Villa Dar es Saada shortly before noon. Chairs were placed on the lawn behind the villa for Roosevelt, Churchill, de Gaulle and Giraud. When they were seated, the official U.S. Army photographers and civilian correspondents (who had been flown from Algiers to Casablanca for the press conference) were admitted. They formed a dense semicircle in front of them.

The president briefed the reporters on the fact that he and the prime minister had met in Casablanca with their Combined Chiefs of Staff to plan the next phase of the war following victory in North Africa, without, however, divulging what strategies were agreed upon.

After a series of meetings, de Gaulle and Giraud agreed to form a National Committee for the Liberation of France, on which they would serve as co-chairmen, with General Giraud in command of the Free French Armed Forces and de Gaulle responsible for political initiatives to unite France against the German occupation.

President Roosevelt asked de Gaulle and Giraud to be photographed with him and Churchill to confirm their agreement to work together. De Gaulle obviously did not want to, but forced by circumstances, did so with an abrupt handshake. Then Sammy Schulman, a civilian war correspondent called out, "I didn't get it, Mr. President." So the president asked de Gaulle and Giraud to shake hands again, which they did to de Gaulle's discomfort.

It was at this press conference that Roosevelt declared that the Allies would accept nothing less than "unconditional surrender" from Germany, Italy and Japan. At this, Churchill looked startled. Apparently, Roosevelt had not mentioned this to him in advance.

The scope and implications of the decisions reached at Casablanca are described in the following joint message which President Roosevelt and Prime Minister Churchill sent to Premier Stalin a week later:

1. We have been in conference with our military advisors and have decided on the operations which are to be undertaken by the American and British forces in the first nine months of 1943. We wish to inform you of our intentions at once. We believe that these operations, together with your powerful offensive, may well bring Germany to her knees in 1943. Every effort must be made to accomplish this purpose.

2. We are in no doubt that our correct strategy is to concentrate on the defeat of Germany with a view to achieving an early and decisive

Generals Giraud and de Gaulle shake hands to confirm their intent to work together.

victory in the European theater. At the same time we must maintain sufficient pressure on Japan to retain the initiative in the Pacific and the Far East and sustain China and prevent the Japanese from extending their aggression to other theaters such as your Maritime Provinces.

3. Our main desire has been to divert strong German land and air forces from the Russian front and to send Russia the maximum flow of supplies. We shall spare no exertion to send you material assistance in any case by every available route.

4. Our immediate intention is to clear the Axis out of North Africa and set up naval and air installations to open:

(1) an effective passage through the Mediterranean for military traffic, and

(2) an intensive bombardment of important Axis targets in Southern Europe.

5. We have made the decision to launch large-scale amphibious operations in the Mediterranean at the earliest possible moment. The preparations for these operations are now under way and will involve a considerable concentration of forces, including landing craft and shipping, in Egypt and the North African ports. In addition, we shall concentrate within the United Kingdom a strong land and air force. These, combined with the British Forces in the United Kingdom, will prepare themselves to re-enter the continent of Europe as soon as practicable. These concentrations will certainly be known to our enemies but they will not know where or when or on what scale we propose striking. They will, therefore, be compelled to divert both land and air forces to all the shores of France, the Low Countries, Corsica, Sardinia, Sicily and the Levant, and Italy, Yugoslavia, Greece, Crete and the Dodecanese.

6. In Europe we shall increase the Allied bomber offensive from the United Kingdom against Germany at a rapid rate and by mid-summer it should be double its present strength. Our experiences to date have shown that day bombing attacks result in the destruction of, and damage to, large numbers of German fighter aircraft. We believe that an increased tempo and weight of daylight and night attacks will lead to greatly increased material and moral damage in Germany and rapidly deplete German fighter strength. As you are aware, we are already containing more than half the German Air Force in Western Europe and the Mediterranean. We have no doubt that our intensi-fied and diversified bombing offensive, together with other operations which we are undertaking, will compel further withdrawal of German air and other forces from the Russian front.

7. In the Pacific it is our intention to eject the Japanese from Rabaul within the next few months and thereafter to exploit the success in the general direction of Japan. We also intend to increase the scale of our operations in Burma in order to reopen this channel of supply to China. We intend to increase our Air Forces in China at once. We shall not, however, allow our offensives against Japan to jeopardize our capacity to take advantage of every opportunity that may present itself for the decisive defeat of Germany in 1943.

8. Our ruling purpose is to bring to bear on Germany and Italy the maximum forces by land, sea and air which can be physically applied.

This message didn't please Stalin, who was impatiently waiting for an imminent announcement that the Allies would invade the mainland of Europe across the English Channel in early 1943. The pitched, prolonged and costly battle of Stalingrad had severely depleted Russian troop strength. In his acknowledgment of Roosevelt and Churchill's report of the results of the Casablanca Conference, he had this to say:

> *Your friendly joint message reached me on January 27. Thank you for informing me of the Casablanca decisions about the operations to be undertaken by the U.S. and British armed forces in the first nine months of 1943. Assuming that your decisions on Germany are designed to defeat her by opening a second front in Europe in 1943, I should be grateful if you would inform me of the concrete operations planned and of their timing. As to the Soviet Union, I can assure you that the Soviet armed forces will do all in their power to continue the offensive against Germany and her allies on the Soviet–German front. We expect to finish our winter campaign, circumstances permitting, in the first half of February. Our troops are tired, they are in need of rest and they will hardly be able to carry on the offensive beyond that period.*

On February 1st, two days after Stalin sent this message, the Germans surrendered at Stalingrad, marking the turning point in Russia's war against Germany.

With the objectives of the conference attained, we left Casablanca immediately after the press conference for a day's rest in Marrakech, on Prime Minister Churchill's recommendation, stopping en route for a picnic lunch by the side of the road. As we lunched, Dad told me that he had talked to the president, who had given me permission to stay on in North Africa.

When we arrived in Marrakech, we were put up in Taylor Villa, a luxurious Moorish-style palace owned by the widow of an American millionaire named Moses Taylor. In her absence, she had arranged to install Kenneth Pendar, the U.S. Vice-Consul, in the villa as a measure of security against vandalism.

We had no sooner arrived than Randolph Churchill insisted that we go immediately to the market for a sight we would never forget. There we found a huge area dominated by a centuries-old minaret. Here were snake charmers, acrobats and storytellers amidst a huge throng. Around the sides were stands selling merchandise and handicrafts of all descriptions. The snake charmer lured what was unmistakably a cobra from its basket, picked it up, and despite my protest, pressed it against my forehead, saying this would bring me good luck. My forehead itched for two days afterwards. I learned that the remarkable acrobats not only spoke English, but were on vacation from their annual performance with Ringling Brothers Barnum & Bailey Circus. During the winter months, they travelled throughout Morocco, performing at one market after another. The storytellers were encircled by a loyal audience. Their stories, with variations in the plot, always had the same characters: a Muslim, a Jew and a Christian. They were dramatically recounted, leading to a suspenseful situation at which point the storyteller would stop and pass the hat. He would not resume the story until his rapt listeners contributed enough money. This centuries-old tradition is the basis for television soap operas in America.

We returned to the Taylor Villa and all went up to the tower to watch the spectacular sunset over the Atlas Mountains. That evening, Kenneth Pendar hosted the farewell dinner with President Roosevelt on his right and Prime Minister Churchill on his left. Other guests were my father, Averell Harriman, Randolph Churchill, Tommy Thompson, and me.

Early the following morning, I said goodbye to the president and thanked him for permitting me to cover the Casablanca Conference. I embraced my father, took my leave of Prime Minister Churchill, then flew back to Algiers with Averell Harriman.

CHAPTER 6

HIATUS

A war correspondent named Dan De Luce approached me a few days after I returned to Algiers. He said he had just received a wire from *Life* magazine asking him to get in touch with me to see if I would write an informal article on the Casablanca Conference for *Life* magazine, reporting sidelights not reported in the newspapers.

I wired my father for approval, which he gave me, then settled down to put my thoughts on paper. The article was published on March 8, 1943 after it had been approved by G-2 and the White House. It was my first effort at writing professionally.

Unrelenting rains in Tunisia had bogged down military operations there. The roads were in such poor condition that supplies to our troops had to be sent by sea. I waited in Algiers for my next assignment.

With the war nearly over in North Africa, it was rumored that the next action would be against Sicily. An assault training program was being offered in Oran and I immediately signed up for it.

It was an arduous, vigorous program, far tougher than anything I had experienced in training in the United States. We went through incredibly difficult obstacle courses in day and night exercises. To add realism as we crawled over rough terrain, a sergeant swept machine gun fire three feet over us, using live ammunition, which kept us close to the ground. While vaulting down from a 12-foot wall, I landed badly and sprained my ankle, eliminating me from the assault on Sicily. I returned to Algiers to recover. Because I could only hobble around on crutches, I was given a desk job at Allied Force Headquarters, where again I served as liaison between AFHQ and our photographic unit in Algiers. It was fully two and a half months before I was declared fit for active duty in the field.

I gave up my room in downtown Algiers and rented a room in a large apartment on Rue Admiral Lyautey, which was closer to our film laboratory and to Allied Force Headquarters at the St. George Hotel. It was more expensive than my first lodgings, but the rent included meals.

The apartment was owned by Captain Petit, a French army officer who was in Morocco on assignment. Madame Petit had three teenage children, two boys and a girl. They spoke little English and were determined to improve my French. Their technique was to refuse to respond if I spoke to them in English. The French I had learned so painfully at Mount Hermon School began to come back to me. Little by little, they broadened my vocabulary and improved my pronunciation and grammar. I began to feel much more at ease in speaking the language.

Bob Murphy invited me to dinner at his apartment overlooking the port of Algiers. Here I met Jean Monnet for the first time. This modest French businessman worked on the Munitions Allocation Board, of which my father was chairman. Dad was so impressed with Monnet's competence and drive that at the Casablanca Conference he urged the president to send him to Algiers to work with Bob Murphy and General Giraud in allocating Lend-Lease supplies to the French army. I was interested to meet this intelligent and self-effacing man, whose respect and admiration for my father seemed to be unbounded.

In the course of the dinner, Jean Monnet revealed that General Giraud had signed a document relinquishing his command of the Free French Forces, despite his pact with General de Gaulle at the Casablanca Conference. This had the effect of turning full command, both political and military, of the Free French Forces over to de Gaulle. Bob Murphy was stunned and dismayed by this development, but there was nothing that could be done to alter it.

A few days later I had dinner with Robert Sherwood, the director of the Office of War Information (OWI), who was on an official visit to Algiers. He told me that the president and my father had watched a screening in the White House of the film I shot at the Casablanca Conference. Bob said he didn't see it himself, but Dad and the president told him they were very pleased by it.

Before the war, Sherwood was a highly successful playwright. When he brought his play "There Shall Be No Night" to Washington for its pre-Broadway opening, he sent two tickets to my father, who had never met him. Dad attended the play. Afterwards he met Sherwood and they talked at some length. Sherwood expressed interest in coming into the government in some capacity. My father later mentioned Sherwood to President Roosevelt, suggesting that he might be a good speechwriter for the President. Roosevelt concurred and Sherwood went on board in that capacity, working closely with my father and the president throughout the war. Before I went overseas, Dad took me to meet Bob Sherwood and his actress wife, Madeline, at a dinner in their Sutton Place apartment.

After my father died in 1946, Sherwood wrote the definitive book on his career entitled *Roosevelt and Hopkins: An Intimate History*. This book, which was based on my father's voluminous papers, was hailed as the most authoritative account of World War II.

Finally, in mid-April 1943, I was assigned to Constantine with a small photography unit having the mundane task of photographing soldiers for new identification cards. We must have taken thousands of pictures before the project was inexplicably cancelled five weeks later.

There was no fighting in that area, so after my work was done for the day, I had ample time to explore that picturesque city. Gasoline was in short supply so the only means of transportation was by horse-drawn coach (a remnant of the 19th century), by bicycle, or by trolley car. Constantine's houses with orange-red tiled roofs were perched high on a cliff surrounded by a deep ravine. When Alexander the Great swept through North Africa it was the only city he could not conquer. The inhabitants defended themselves simply by demolishing the only bridge over the ravine leading to the city and Alexander passed it by. I saw the remains of the ancient stone bridge still at the bottom of the ravine.

On May 8th, the Allies began their occupation of Tunis. I raced to Tunis to film the victory parade led by General George C. Marshall, astride a magnificent white horse. An estimated 200,000 Germans and Italians had been encircled, captured or killed in the campaign. Huge quantities of war materials fell into our hands. They were catalogued and photographed for the War Department. Like the identification card photographs, this was a tedious job.

My next assignment was with a photo unit located on a clifftop in Tunisia. There were six of us in this unit under the command of a lieutenant. We were billeted in a farmhouse high above the town of Le Kef (the Arab term for cliff). It had been constructed on the site of 14 Roman farms, where I found shards of ancient Roman pottery.

Our lieutenant would check regularly with the intelligence unit at regional headquarters and assign us to cover stories of interest. In the months that followed I travelled widely in Tunisia, filming subjects from Kasserine Pass, where American forces had suffered a stunning defeat by the Germans in February, and to Gafsa, Gabes, Sfax and Sousse.

CHAPTER 7

ITALY: SALERNO TO MONTE CASSINO

I applied to my regimental commander for permission to cover the next military operation, which I assumed would be a major invasion of Italy. He promised to include my name in the photographic teams he was assembling. There were still very few of us official photographers and cameramen in North Africa, although we had heard that more were being trained in the United States for assignment abroad. Nine of us—five still photographers and four motion picture cameramen—were selected for the landings in southern Italy under the command of Lieutenant Benson. In due course, we were sent to a staging area in Tunisia.

I was issued a 35-mm Eyemo motion picture camera with three lenses mounted on a turret, a tripod and 1,000 feet of film in cans of 100 feet each. In addition, I carried a carbine, cartridge belt, gas mask and the full field pack of an infantryman.

It was clear to us that the invasion of Italy would not be like the placid debarkation we experienced in Algiers. In our final briefings, we were told that we would land near the ancient town of Paestum in the Gulf of Salerno. Our landing craft would bring us within wading distance of the beach under the cover of darkness. We were told to expect stiff resistance from the enemy.

Because we would be wading ashore, we were ordered to protect our photographic equipment from water damage. I loaded my camera with film, covered the lenses with army-issued condoms, then enveloped the entire camera with a plastic bag securely taped shut. I packed the remaining film in plastic and put it in a canvas bag strapped to my belt.

The night was mild and the sea was calm for our voyage across the Mediterranean. We were aboard a large launch which had been converted to a landing craft by the addition of a ramp on either side of the bow. These would be lowered when we reached shallow water for our debarkation. To our right, left and behind us were hundreds of other landing craft of various descriptions, together with larger U.S. Navy vessels. It was evident that we were going to be part of the first wave of invaders.

Although initially the voyage seemed serene, tension rose as we approached the Italian coastline. Then, unexpectedly, came the announcement that the Italians had surrendered. The news made us catch our breath. Perhaps the landing would be an easy one after all.

There was no sign of the enemy as our landing craft approached the shore and the ramps were lowered. I was on the starboard side and I carefully watched the men as they went down the ramp on the port side. As predicted, they entered waist-deep water. Relieved at this, I confidently went down the ramp on my side of the boat, only to plunge into water well over my head. Although weighed down with all my equipment, I somehow struggled to the surface, and managed to get my footing.

Then, abruptly, the racket of machine gun and cannon fire exploded from the shore. Streams of tracer bullets streaked out at us. The Italians had surrendered, but the Germans certainly had not. They were grimly waiting for us. I clumsily made my way to the beach, and the nine of us assembled. We marched all night under fire, but we were still on the beach as the sky lightened. When the night faded into day, I could see the silhouette of the Greek Temple of Health at Paestum high on the hill above our landing beach. Gunfire intensified as visibility improved and we could see how many men had fallen on the beach under that intense barrage. Over to our left there was an artillery duel between a German Tiger tank concealed in the woods and an American destroyer just off shore.

Our tanks and other vehicles were making their way ashore as it became light enough for us to begin photographing and filming the scene.

On the beach, there was a jeep that had hit a mine. Its steel floor had been blow upwards in jagged points. There was no sign of its occupants. I filmed a distant establishing shot, then moved in for a medium shot, and finally climbed aboard the jeep for a close-up.

A sergeant shouted to me, "Hey bud, how did you get out there?"

"I just walked out," I replied.

"Well, let's see you just walk back. That area hasn't been cleared of mines!"

I looked back in dismay, searching vainly for my footsteps so I could retrace the path I had taken to the jeep, but all the indentations in the sand looked alike. After long deliberation and an ardent prayer, I took a deep breath and walked back to safety. The mines on the beach were anti-tank mines, not anti-personnel mines.

We were divided into three-man photo teams consisting of a still photographer, a motion picture cameraman and a driver for the jeep which was issued to each team. We were instructed to contact the intelligence officer in a corps or division to determine which units were in contact with the enemy and to then attach ourselves to it to film the action which followed. When that unit was relieved, we would join their replacement or move off to another sector of the front. This meant we were in action every day and most nights.

Air support from Sicily and Tunisia, combined with the advance of our armored units, gradually forced back the Germans. They, however, made our progress as costly as possible by mining the roads and by concealing anti-personnel booby traps in their barricades. They planted "S" mines everywhere. These had a 3-pronged trigger which barely emerged from the earth and was almost invisible. If an unfortunate soldier stepped on it, there would be a small explosion which projected a canister waist high in the air. Then the canister would explode with a major blast which was designed to disable rather than kill. The Germans operated on the premise that it was more costly to us to have three people care for a wounded soldier than for one soldier to die.

As a quick and effective way of barricading the roads, the Germans placed plastic explosives around a half-dozen tree trunks and set them off so that the trees fell across the road. Then they hid booby traps in the branches, which were wired to explode when we tried to move the trees out of the way. Not only were all the roads mined, the pastures and lightly wooded areas were mined as well, in the event we attempted to bypass a barricade.

I remember one incident when an officer, eager to get his troops around a barricade, decided to lead them across an open field. There were no demolition experts available to clear the mines, so he drove a flock of sheep across the field. The sheep effectively cleared a safe passage at the cost of their lives.

Demolition experts in the Army Engineers were kept busy clearing the mines and booby traps so we could move forward. On foot, they would head a column of our tanks, locating mines with electronic mine sweepers. They used a bayonet to dig them up, then disarmed them. It was an agonizing, slow process that made a mockery of our swift mechanized army. When they cleared a path, they would lay down white cloth tapes on either side to delineate the cleared area. Sometimes, at night, the Germans would stealthily move one of the tapes so that the path then marked out was still sown with mines.

I spent a week with a unit of these courageous men, filming a story on their dangerous task. It was nervous work for me just filming them as they plunged their bayonets into the earth. They seemed to know how much pressure to use to dig up a mine without exploding it. Their casualties were high, but the army showed its respect for their work by granting them senior non-commissioned rank. Most of them were master sergeants.

After we broke out of the beachhead, I attached my team to an infantry outfit and we moved with it into the town of Salerno, which had suffered serious damage from the artillery before our arrival. I filmed the advance of our troops through the town as they went from house to house to ensure that the enemy was not lurking there. The Germans had withdrawn just before we arrived. The local inhabitants were nowhere to be seen.

We moved on to Avellino. Here we had the heady experience of being the first American troops to liberate a major Italian city. We were greeted with shouts of joy, flowers, bottles of wine, and embraces from men and women alike. I filmed it all.

We paused here and were immediately surrounded by jubilant Italians. Some, who spoke English, asked us where we were from in America, then pressed us for information about their brothers or cousins who had settled in New York or Chicago, apparently assuming that we must know them.

The infantry moved on in pursuit of the retreating Germans. We stuck with the advance units. In Benevento, we were again the first American troops to arrive and we were treated to similar frenzied welcomes. The local brass band was assembled and played for us and the mayor gave a speech in Italian littered with words and phrases in English.

We were exhilarated but exhausted when we arrived in Caserta to yet another tumultuous but joyous welcome. Again, we were greeted with flowers, shouts of welcome, warm embraces, proffered bottles of wine, and invitations to dinner.

Our first thought was to find a base headquarters for ourselves. As we drove through the city, we discovered the magnificent Queen's

Palace and immediately occupied it. We had only a few hours to enjoy it before the British roared into town in force. They outranked us and firmly told us we had to find other quarters.

Nearby, we found a spacious modern home with a large garden in front. It had been the winter home of a wealthy fascist farm leader. The Germans had occupied it shortly before we arrived, using it as some kind of headquarters. We discovered that they had tunnelled deep under the front garden, creating a huge underground shelter with emergency exits concealed on the surface by large wooden flower boxes. They had to retreat before they had an opportunity to reinforce the walls and ceiling with concrete. In a niche in the wall, I found a dozen or so small glass vials containing a clear liquid. I took them to the army engineers, who immediately recognized them as nitroglycerine detonators. I gladly relinquished the vials to them.

We used Caserta for a base of operations. It was good to be in a house with running water, modern plumbing and comfortable beds.

I heard about a firefight involving a U.S. infantry unit which had just arrived in Italy. I went up to cover the story, only to learn that the action was precipitated in the middle of the night when a nervous sentry in Company A imagined he spotted a German in the vicinity, challenged him and fired his rifle. Company B responded immediately with gunfire and a brief but pitched battle ensued in the dark. Fortunately, no one was killed or injured.

I also filmed a feature story on the highly-decorated Japanese-American battalion which had fought with such distinction in the Italian campaign.

Major Ransom moved up to Caserta and we turned the house over to him for his headquarters. He ordered Lieutenant Benson to set up an advance headquarters farther up the line. I was promoted to sergeant.

Southern Italy had not had any rainfall for some weeks before the landing. The hard-packed dirt roads were ground into clouds of fine dust by our tanks, half-tracks and trucks, clotting our eyes and nostrils and coating our throats. Then heavy rains transformed the dusty roads into deep muddy bogs, slowing our advance. As the fall changed to winter, temperatures fell and snow covered the mountains in which we found ourselves. The muddy roads froze the ruts in place, making driving difficult and dangerous. Sure-footed mules were brought in to carry munitions and supplies to our advance outposts.

We moved northward along the Volturno River.

I attached myself to an artillery outfit that had orders to clear the enemy out of a village just over the crest of the mountain. I had been briefed on the time when the artillery barrage would begin, so I posted myself on the mountaintop in advance to film the early morning activities of the village.

It was a small, poor place composed of farming families who scratched out a living by cultivating the steep slopes of the mountain. Smoke rose from a few chimney pots. There were two or three women in the street. I saw no evidence of German troops there.

Suddenly, the first shell was fired. It was a phosphorus "marker" shell that set up a plume of white smoke. It landed disturbingly close to me on my side of the mountain crest. The artillery officer had neglected to tell me about that. Then came salvo after salvo of shells that whooshed over my head and rained down on the village, enveloping it in smoke and dust. The attack lasted only about fifteen minutes, but when the smoke cleared, I could see that nearly every building had been hit and the village was virtually demolished.

I moved down to what was left of it, and filmed the few shocked survivors who tentatively emerged from the vestiges of their homes. Women who had been out on errands just minutes before lay dead on the street, their bodies covered with rubble and dust.

An hour later I filmed a stony-faced woman bearing a coffin on her head, doubtless containing the body of her child. She picked her way carefully down the mountainside toward the small cemetery. By this time, I had been joined by a civilian war correspondent who, years before, covered the rape of Nanking. He also filmed the woman with the coffin. When she headed down toward the cemetery, he ordered her to go back up the hill and she stoically complied. When I challenged him about this, he said, "It'll make a more dramatic picture if she is climbing uphill, instead of down."

I still don't understand how anyone could be so heartless.

I was sickened by this whole affair. The town had been destroyed for no reason. The enemy was not there.

The Germans, however, took note of our artillery position and, in an attack that lasted for forty-eight hours they blanketed us with a deafening barrage of artillery shells. Our casualties were heavy. While I filmed this counterattack, a soldier next to me said, "This is nothing—you should have been here yesterday."

"I *was* here yesterday," I replied.

He seemed to think that we went back to some safe haven after filming the action.

Lieutenant Benson joined me and said he had received a message from Washington stating that Americans were slacking off in buying war bonds because with our initial victories in Italy they felt the war was going well for us. The War Department ordered combat cameramen and photographers to take pictures of wounded and dead American soldiers to show the sacrifices that American soldiers continue to make in Italy.

I complied, but it was my worst assignment in the entire war.

After the battle of the Volturno, the mode of fighting in the Italian theater changed considerably. Instead of setting up lines of strong resistance in the mountains or in towns, the Germans began retreating with amazing rapidity. They maintained a rear guard delaying action until bridges could be blown up and roads blocked by trees, or in the case of towns, by rubble. Often, the Germans didn't have time to set off their charges and we found their explosives still attached to trees and bridges. These were disarmed by the engineers and we advanced unimpeded.

The Germans were apparently under the impression that we were short of food. As they retreated, they destroyed farms, leaving cattle dead and bloated in the fields. They burned haystacks to prevent us from sleeping in them. We also discovered that they took time to conceal booby traps in houses they left standing. Their favorite hiding places for these insidious devices were bedsprings and toilets. Mines, booby traps and terrible weather were our main obstacles as we pushed the Germans farther and farther north.

On November 1, 1943, in a special exchange arrangement with British 10th Corps in Italy, I was assigned to cover the military action of the British 56th Division commanded by Major General Templar. My partner was an English cameraman named Freddy Mott. In the 17 days that followed, we filmed a Scottish battalion entering Teano in street-fighting formation, smashing in doors of houses in the search for Germans. After they secured and occupied Teano, they moved on to Rocca where a British concert party called the Cat's Whiskers entertained the men of the 56th Division with music and song just a few miles from German lines. I had never seen our own USO entertainers that close to the front.

We filmed a German observation post being shelled by a British artillery unit which fought in the British 8th Army against General Rommel in the long trek from El Alamein to Tunis. The guns were badly in need of reboring. Nevertheless, they fired effectively. The Germans returned fire in an artillery duel that went on unabated for two days and nights. We got little sleep.

In the vicinity of the monastery on the summit of Monte Cassino, I filmed a meeting between Major General Templar and the U.S. Major General L.K. Truscott, Jr. as they discussed the problem of securing the strategic high point of the Monte Cassino Monastery. The unresolved question was whether or not the Germans actually occupied the monastery. We knew they were in the area because we could see the glare of their windshields as they drove along the winding road leading up to Monte Cassino.

I offered to film the monastery using my telephoto lens. This could provide a graphic document proving that the Nazis were using the monastery as an observation post. General Truscott rejected my proposal, saying that the area was heavily mined and I would never be able to get up and back alive.

Mott and I entered the deserted mountain village of Roccamonfina, which had been evacuated by its inhabitants when the Germans occupied it. Timidly, a few of the inhabitants emerged from the forest. One of these was a watchmaker with a briefcase full of watches, which he offered for sale. I selected an Omega chronometer which he sold to me for $75. It served me well throughout the rest of the war, helping me calculate the distance from which artillery was firing at us and also helping me verify the speed of my camera motor, which tended to slow down in very cold weather.

On November 17th, I returned to our advance headquarters to send my exposed film to the War Department and to replenish my stock of film. Lieutenant Benson ordered me to report immediately to our headquarters in Caserta. Here, Colonel Gillette, who had been my commanding officer at the studio in Astoria, informed me that I must leave as soon as possible for Naples to catch a flight to Tunis on a priority basis. He said this was a special assignment and I should take enough film for an entire month. In addition to shooting motion picture film, I was also to be prepared to take still pictures. I was issued a Speed Graphic camera, a Contax 35-mm camera and a 16-mm Filmo, with which I could film in color.

Colonel Gillette surmised that this could be an assignment to cover another conference, although he had no official confirmation of this. He said I must report to the advanced Allied Force Headquarters (AFHQ) in Tunis by the 19th of the month at the latest. He told me that when I completed the assignment, I was to report to Algiers, because replacement photographers from the States were arriving and he could relieve those of us who had covered the Italian campaign since the landings at Salerno.

During the Italian campaign, Robert Hopkins was promoted to sergeant.

As I said goodbye Colonel Gillette, he told me that my commanding officer, Major Arthur Ransom was recommending me for the Legion of Merit for my action under fire for 69 days in Italy. Months later, I learned that General Truscott declined to approve the recommendation, saying, "Hopkins was just doing his duty." Since I have never seen the established standards for the award of the Legion of Merit, I can only assume that General Truscott was correct in his judgement.

It was only when I was demobilized from the army that I was given my own 201 Personnel File and I was able to read Major Ransom's recommendation for myself. It read:

CONFIDENTIAL

DETACHMENT #1
2625th Signal Service Regiment
APO # 306

27 November 1943

SUBJECT: Legion of Merit Award
TO : CG, NATOUSE, APO 534 (Thru Channels)

1. Under the provisions of Section IV, War Department Circular 131, dated 3 June 1943, It is recommended that T/4 Robert NMI Hopkins, 32183182, of this detachment be considered for the award of the Legion of Merit.

2. I have personal knowledge of the facts hereinafter stated and I am of the opinion that these facts reveal that T/4 Hopkins has performed outstanding services which distinguish him above men of like grade or experience and that his achievements merit the recommended award.

3. Detailed description of the services rendered:

T/4 Hopkins was a motion picture cameraman selected to participate in the Operation AVALANCHE and secure motion pictures of combat and other phases of the operation. He landed with the 57th Signal Battalion on the beaches of Paestum, Italy, on D-Day 9 September 1943. Throughout, his work was characterized by aggressive and courageous action. On numerous occasions he exposed himself to enemy fire to secure exceptional motion pictures. In one instance, reminded of the extreme hazard of his position, he replied that he had full knowledge of its dangers but could find no other location so well suited to his needs at the time.

He consistently operated with the leading elements of the infantry and on many occasions was among the first to enter a newly-won city or town. This was especially fine at Avellino and the films he made there were unusually valuable because the city was the first one of considerable size to be captured by American troops. The excellence of his work is indicated by the fact that he received commendation from the War Department, Commanding General NATOUSA, Commanding General FIFTH ARMY and Commanding General VI Corps.

After credibly completing missions in the zones of every American infantry Division involved in the operation, he was selected for temporary duty with the British X Corps. British officers with whom he served spoke most highly of his initiative, courage, resourcefulness, and soldierly demeanor.

Although fundamentally a motion picture cameraman, he was continually alert to the more prosaic needs of his unit and made frequent reports of such matters as possible future locations for the unit's headquarters or bivouac area. T/4 Hopkins, by act and example, contributed greatly to the successful performance of his unit's mission.

Period of time involved: 9 September 1943 to 17 November 1943.

(Signed)
ARTHUR K. RANSOM,
Major, Signal Corps,
Commanding

General Truscott's formal endorsement read as follows:

CONFIDENTIAL
HEADQUARTERS VI CORPS, APO 306, U.S. ARMY

6 April 1944

1. Not favorably considered.
2. The services described indicate a fine performance of duty but it is not felt that they are of such character as to justify the award of the Legion of Merit.

(Signed)
L.K. TRUSCOTT, JR.
Major General, U.S. Army

I left Caserta on the afternoon of November 17th, traveling by jeep with two other men, both strangers to me, toward Naples. It was a clear, cold day with the temperature well below freezing. Endless columns of refugees trudged along both sides of the road, some going toward Naples, others going in the opposite direction. They were burdened with all the personal belongings they could carry or wheel along as they sought refuge from their destroyed homes.

We were slowed by the heavy traffic when I saw a scene so surreal that I couldn't interpret its meaning at first. Up ahead, high above us, suspended from the bare branch of a tree, was a cartwheel. Further up was a high-button shoe and a piece of fabric. Then it dawned on me that refugees in a two-wheeled cart had run over a mine which exploded, flinging fragments of the cart, its contents and its occupants skyward.

Off to the left, in a pasture below the embankment, we saw the nude body of a young girl. She was lying on her back with one arm under her head and the other flung out to her side. She had long blonde hair. Her blue eyes gazed placidly up at the cloudless sky. She was about 16 years old.

We parked the jeep and hurried to her side. She obviously had been killed instantly by the concussion from the mine, which also stripped her of her clothes. There was not a scratch, a bruise or any mark on her to suggest she had died violently. Rigor mortis had set in.

Vultures were circling overhead and we knew we had to bury her. Because we couldn't bend her outstretched arm, we traced the outline of her body on the earth and gently moved it to one side. We didn't have a shovel so we frantically tried to use the lids of our mess kits to loosen the unyielding, hard-frozen earth. One of my companions sobbed as we worked, saying over and over again, "She could be my sister!"

CHAPTER 8

THE CAIRO CONFERENCE

I saw Commander Harry Butcher, General Eisenhower's naval aide, on November 20th. He confirmed that Dad would be arriving with President Roosevelt in the afternoon. I was ordered to the "White House" at 1:30 (I learned that anywhere the president stayed was called the White House).

Dad arrived an hour later. He looked exhausted and not at all well. But it was wonderful to see him and he seemed both surprised and happy to see me. He told me that the president was going to meet Generalissimo Chiang Kai-Shek and Winston Churchill, along with their respective Chiefs of Staff, in Cairo. The Cairo Conference would focus on the war in the Pacific. After the conference in Cairo, Roosevelt and Churchill would meet Marshall Stalin in Teheran. Dad said I was to remain with the president's party to cover both conferences.

General Marshall, President Roosevelt, General Spaatz, General Eisenhower, Sir Charles Portal, Air Marshal Tedder and Admirals Leahy and King arrived shortly after my father. Elliott and Franklin Roosevelt Jr. accompanied by two young women—Kay Summersby, who was General Eisenhower's chauffeur, and Nancy Gatch from the Red Cross—joined the group.

At the president's request, I took some personal "family" pictures of the president, Dad, Elliott and Franklin on the patio outside the villa which served as General Eisenhower's quarters.

The following morning, General Marshall, Admiral King, Air Marshal Tedder and Sir Charles Portal flew on to Cairo. Then General Eisenhower conducted a tour for the president and his party, including me, of Medjez-el-Bab and Tebourba, the scene of very

*A family picture of Col. Elliott Roosevelt, Harry Hopkins, Commander Franklin
D. Roosevelt, Jr., and President Roosevelt on November 20, 1943 taken on the
patio of General Eisenhower's villa in Carthage near Tunis.*

heavy fighting during the African campaign. He explained the
various phases of the war as we moved along. I was able to describe
to my father my own experiences in this sector during the conflict.
We had lunch on the road and returned to the "White House" late in
the afternoon.

We boarded C-54 transport planes at 10:30 P.M. to fly to
Cairo. The president, Dad and Admiral Leahy took plane number
one. I was in plane number two with several of the Secret Service
men. We were all pretty tired and went to sleep almost immediately.

When I awoke the next morning, the sky was just lightening in
the east. We were flying over the Sahara Desert. As I watched, the
sun rose, casting an eerie red glow across the endless dunes of the
desert. It was the most bleak, barren landscape I have ever seen.
There was neither vegetation nor habitation as far at I could see.
Nothing but empty desert. It seemed almost as if we had flown to
the moon overnight. More than any story or film, it made me
appreciate what a terrible ordeal the British 8th Army must have
endured in the campaign from El Alamein to Tunis.

We arrived in Cairo at 7:10 in the morning. The president's
plane was nowhere to be seen, although it had left Tunis ten

Harry Hopkins and Ambassador John Winant at the entrance to Kirk Villa in Cairo on November 21, 1943.

minutes ahead of us. I later learned that Roosevelt had asked the pilot to fly up the Nile Valley and over the Valley of the Kings so that he and his party could see the remarkable monuments of that ancient civilization.

In Cairo, the president, Dad, Admiral Leahy, and the president's son-in-law, Major John Boettinger, were installed in the Kirk Villa, a home belonging to Alexander Kirk, the American Ambassador to Egypt. The house was located in the area of the Mena House Hotel and had an unobstructed view of the Pyramids

Harry and Robert Hopkins photographed in front of the Sphinx on November 23, 1943.

and the Sphinx about a mile away. The Mena House was reserved for the conference in Cairo.

Prime Minister Churchill and his party, including his daughter, Sarah Oliver, arrived a day ahead of us and were installed a couple of miles away from the president's quarters.

Since everyone was spending the rest of the day getting organized and there would be no pictures for me to take, I went to my billet, a villa two houses away from the Kirk Villa. There I took my first hot shower in many months.

The next afternoon, at about four o'clock, the prime minister arrived at Kirk Villa. I filmed him as he came up the walk. He loomed ever-larger in my view finder until I put down my camera and he grasped my hand in greeting. He had come to invite the president and his party for a tour of the Pyramids.

We chatted for a few minutes and we were joined by General Smuts. I was surprised that he remembered me from the tour of the defenses of Dover a year earlier. Churchill told me that during the Boer War, when he had been a newspaper reporter, General Smuts had put him in prison as a spy. I was tempted to tell the prime minister that the British army had put me in jail for the same reason in Tunisia, but I decided I had better not since the soldiers were only doing their job and Churchill might have taken some action against them.

When Churchill went into the villa to see the president, General Smuts took me to one side and said, "Sergeant, you're in a unique position. Remember everything you see and hear. It will influence your life forever."

And so it has.

I was rushing around taking pictures of Roosevelt and Churchill with both my Speed Graphic and my Eyemo, so I didn't have much of a chance to see the Pyramids myself. I wanted to get a picture of the president with the Sphinx in the background, but I couldn't because the president remained seated in the car which had been driven out onto the sand.

The prime minister enlisted the aid of a native guide to explain the history of the Pyramids and the Sphinx. When he finished, the guide refused to take the gratuity offered by a member of the Secret Service. The prime minister learned of this and he went over to the guide to press a tip on him. The guide bowed low but still refused the money. The prime minister asked if he knew to whom he had been giving his lecture. Again the guide bowed low and said, "Yes *Sahib*, I knew, but not properly." The prime minister smiled and returned to his car.

Security was tight, but almost everyone in Cairo knew that something important was going on. This guide, at least, knew who some of the principals were.

I asked the guide if he would take a picture of my father and me in front of the Sphinx with the Great Pyramid in the background. I handed him my Speed Graphic and showed him which button to push. He gladly obliged and accepted the tip I offered.

Dad and I went over to the Great Pyramid. There a wizened, elderly Egyptian wagered ten shillings that he could beat me in a race to the top of the pyramid. Eager to show my father the fact that my muscles had hardened during the campaign in Italy, I accepted the wager. We each gave my father a ten-shilling note to

Generalissimo Chiang Kai-Shek, President Roosevelt and Prime Minister Churchill with their respective Chiefs of Staff at the Cairo Conference where the strategy in the war of the Pacific was determined, on November 24, 1943.

hold and Dad gave the signal to start. The Egyptian was up and away while I was still trying to find a way to clamber up the huge, shoulder-high blocks of stone at the base of the pyramid. Once I found a way, the climb was a somewhat easier, but the Egyptian was nowhere in sight. From the ground I had misjudged the true height of the pyramid. I stubbornly continued to climb. Finally, breathlessly, I reached the summit only to find the Egyptian already there. I shook his hand and sheepishly admitted defeat. Back on the sand, I gave him the two ten-shilling notes. My father soothed my wounded ego by saying that the Egyptian had obviously been climbing the pyramid since he was a little boy and knew the easiest and swiftest way to the top.

On November 24th, President Roosevelt had a conference with the Combined British, Chinese and American Chiefs of Staff and a mixture of ambassadors and ministers. These included Anthony Eden, John Gill Winant, Averell Harriman, Alexander Kirk, and others. British, Chinese and other American military photographers

General Chiang Kai-Shek, President Roosevelt and Prime Minister Winston Churchill at the Cairo Conference on November 24, 1943.

were called in and we all took pictures of the group on the lawn in the back of Kirk Villa. I took both still and motion pictures.

A burly Chinese photographer in civilian clothes kept asking me for the proper exposure for the pictures in the bright Egyptian sun. Before he left, he gave me his card and asked me to call on him when I go to China. According to his card, he was a major general in the Chinese army named J.L. Huang.

The following day was Thanksgiving and no meetings were scheduled. I went to downtown Cairo to do some shopping in the bazaar.

In contrast to the conference compound, the narrow alleys of the bazaar were jammed with people, most in Arab garb. Hawkers from the stands lining the alley grabbed at me, cajoling me to come and see their wares "just for the pleasure of the eyes." Persistent even when I said no, they followed me for a considerable distance, begging me to return to their stands. The goods they offered were enticing: carved sandalwood tables inlaid with mother of pearl, dazzling silks shot with gold thread, ceramics and pots of all descriptions, glittering jewelry, curved swords and daggers encased in silver scabbards.

I emerged with my purchases, some silver and ivory bracelets and necklaces and some silks. I also bought a blue velvet jacket from Damascas. It was a beautiful garment, embroidered in gold and lined in red silk, called a Crusader jacket. It would be a gift for a girl I had yet to meet.

That evening, at President Roosevelt's invitation, I attended Thanksgiving dinner at the Kirk Villa with my father. There were about 15 guests, including Winston Churchill and his daughter, Sara Oliver; John Martin, Churchill's secretary; Averell Harriman; Alexander Kirk; Laurence Steinhardt; Elliott Roosevelt; and Charles (Chip) Bohlen. The Chinese were not represented.

It was a traditional Thanksgiving feast, preceded by cocktails and hors d'oeuvres, with roast turkey and cranberry sauce, sweet potatoes, mashed white potatoes, green peas, pumpkin pie and vanilla ice cream, all accompanied by wine, a welcome change from the field rations I had consumed during the Italian campaign.

There was not enough room at the main table, so Dad, Ambassador Steinhardt and I sat nearby at a small round table. Conversation at our table centered around speculation as to who would command the Allied assault across the English Channel to France. Clearly, not even my father knew who would command that critical venture. The names which surfaced most frequently were General George C. Marshall and General Dwight D. Eisenhower.

When we finished our dessert, President Roosevelt described the origin of Thanksgiving dinner as a local New England custom to celebrate the survival of English settlers there for an entire year under adverse circumstances. The celebration gradually spread throughout the 13 colonies and then, as the nation expanded westward, throughout the nation, becoming a national holiday. Now, with U.S. troops throughout the world, it had become an international holiday.

Turning to Churchill, he said how deeply touched he was to share this traditional holiday with the man who had worked side by side with him in their momentous common struggle. He then proposed a toast to Prime Minister Churchill.

Churchill rose to his feet, saying how proud he was to be permitted to share our holiday with us. His speech was a masterpiece of eloquence and drama. He used no notes and I believe he improvised as he spoke. He began in a low, clear voice, which mounted to a powerful

General Eisenhower receiving the Legion of Merit Medal from President Roosevelt in Cairo on November 26, 1943.

crescendo as he came to the conclusion and proposed a toast to President Roosevelt. But at one point, as he devised a particularly complex sentence which seemed to leave him no word to complete it, he fell silent. It was a silence which seemed to last for a full two minutes. He simply stood there. His expression did not change.

I said to myself, "He's 68 years old, and can no longer craft those pithy and resonant sentences for which he had become renowned." My own vocabulary raced through my mind, but I could find no word to extricate him from this grammatical impasse.

Then, with the flair of a magician, Churchill drew from his extraordinary memory the only word in the English language to fit so precisely in this sentence. It seemed to have been chiselled from crystal to fit this particular situation.

There was an audible sigh of relief from his listeners, who had held their breath in concern. The prime minister then brought his remarks to a close and offered a toast to President Roosevelt.

Winston Churchill had not lost his touch.

It was Dad who broke up the dinner at about eleven o'clock when he found that some of the guests were talking business, something they had done since the conference began. We all moved into the living room where Dad had arranged for a U.S. Army band to play throughout dinner and afterwards. The leader asked for requests. The prime minister was partial to John Philip Sousa's military marches. The band struck up a stirring march immediately. Then Anthony Eden asked the band to play Noel Coward's "We're Going to Hang up the Washing on the Siegfreid Line," but the band didn't know it. Undeterred, the British foreign minister sang it with considerable verve, a capella.

This was the first opportunity I had to meet Sarah Oliver and she and I danced together for several numbers. As she was the only woman present, virtually all the other guests danced with her as well.

The party broke up at one o'clock in the morning. I thanked the president for including me, and retired for the night.

The following morning, General Eisenhower flew into Cairo from Tunis. He had not taken part in the deliberations during the Cairo Conference. The president asked me to photograph his meeting with General Eisenhower, at which time he awarded him the Legion of Merit Medal.

The president asked how many pictures I intended to take.

"Three, Mr. President," I replied.

"All right," he said. "But I don't want you to say afterwards, 'Just one more, Mr. President.'"

As I set up my camera, the president asked Eisenhower how he had arrived in Cairo. Eisenhower replied that he had flown in on a regularly scheduled Military Aircraft Transport System (MATS) flight.

The president scolded him, saying, "You're the supreme commander. You mustn't be limited by a MATS schedule. You are entitled to your own aircraft to take you promptly where you must be. Take care of this as soon as you return to Tunis."

I wondered as I took the pictures if this was President Roosevelt's hint that Eisenhower would be in command of the Normandy invasion. A week later, the suspense was over. Eisenhower was appointed to that command.

My father took me to meet Madame Chiang Kai-Shek, who had invited us to tea. She was a lovely, dainty woman, dressed in a Chinese gown. The Generalissimo was not present. She immediately put me at ease, offering me tea and cake.

She seemed genuinely interested in what I had been doing. She didn't ask questions just to make conversation, but wanted to know in detail the nature of my job. Before we left, she told me to be sure and visit her as soon as I go to China.

CHAPTER 9

THE TEHERAN CONFERENCE

I was in the lead aircraft on the morning of November 27, 1943. We flew for hours over desert and barren mountains, over Suez, the Dead Sea, Jerusalem and Baghdad—all exotic places I had read about. Dad and I were in separate airplanes. Later he remarked that one of the last things he dreamed of was that we would be flying over the Persian Desert together. I photographed the president's arrival at Teheran Airport.

Teheran is right in the middle of the desert, with apparently no economic reason for its presence there except that it is, and has been for some time, the capital of the country. Mountains rise up quite suddenly about 75 miles to the north with the Caspian Sea and Russia on the other side of them. At the time it seemed nothing grew on that parched land and there was no industry.

A large and modern city, Teheran had a population of about 70,000, but there was no water except for that which flowed down the city's gutters from the melting snow on the mountains. Those fortunates who lived in the northern outskirts got clean water for drinking and cooking, but as it made its way down into the city center and beyond it became increasingly polluted.

We were driven to our quarters in the American Legation, but the next afternoon were transferred to a villa inside the compound of the Russian embassy "because of lack of space" in the American Legation. Another explanation given was that Nazi agents had learned the president was in Teheran and Stalin was concerned for his safety in having to make the long trip to and from the conference site through the city. Personally, I thought Stalin wanted Roosevelt in quarters controlled by the Russians. Churchill and the British delegation were lodged in the British embassy nearby.

I was issued a pass, written in Russian, which permitted me access to the Russian embassy compound. I was struck by how well guarded it was. Russian soldiers, all of whom were at least six feet tall, stood at rigid attention for their entire three-hour shift guarding the embassy, moving only to salute.

The grounds of the embassy were alive with NKVD agents. They seemed to spring out of the ground. They wore long black overcoats and peaked caps. Unlike the soldiers, most of the agents were short in stature.

As my father and I made our way across the grounds to the quarters assigned to us, I asked him, "Why are we dealing with the Russians? Russia is a dictatorship and we are a democracy. They don't share our concept of freedom and justice."

""We're helping them," said my father, "because they are holding down 95 Nazi divisions. Without our help to the Russians, the Nazis would be victorious and they would turn those 95 divisions against us. That's why we're dealing with them."

As we were unpacking in our new quarters, I commented that I had seen so much death and destruction during the campaigns in North Africa and Italy that I hoped that someone in Washington was giving some thought to a plan to prevent another war like this.

He replied, "Get your priorities straight. First we have to win this war—then we'll study ways to prevent another."

Roosevelt met with Stalin informally on the afternoon of November 28th, but no photographs were authorized for that meeting.

Mike Reilly told me that I should be prepared to take pictures of a ceremony during the afternoon of November 29th, in which Churchill would present the Sword of Stalingrad on behalf of King George VI and the British people to Stalin commemorating the heroic defense of that city against the Nazi siege.

Following the ceremony, pictures were to be taken of the three leaders—Roosevelt, Churchill and Stalin. These would be significant pictures because they represented the grand alliance of the United States, Great Britain and the Soviet Union.

The Sword of Stalingrad ceremony was held in the ballroom of the Russian embassy. I staked out a good vantage point. The room was filled with allied staff officers and diplomats. I watched Churchill and Stalin as they entered, then looked everywhere for President Roosevelt.

The Sword of Stalingrad ceremony in Teheran on November 29, 1943.

I suddenly realized he was seated right next to me. He had been carried in by Secret Servicemen so tall that they concealed him and no one realized he had entered until he was seated.

I was surprised to see that Stalin, like Churchill, was quite short, measuring about five foot six inches. Interestingly enough, his senior advisors—Molotov, Vishinsky and Voroshilov—who were standing nearby, were the same height as Stalin, which suggested that he did not want any of those close to him to tower over him.

Stalin's hair and moustache were grey. He had calm, clear eyes. He wore a simple military uniform with two stars on his epaulets and a single medal, the Red Star of Russia, on his chest. He appeared to be a soldier from head to foot.

The Russian band played the three national anthems and the ceremony began. Churchill read from a scroll extolling the courage of the Russian people in turning back the Nazis who had held the city of Stalingrad in siege, and thereby turned the tide of war in Russia's favor.

The sword, which was held aloft by a British officer, had been forged for the occasion by the Wilkinson Sword Company. It was a beautiful object. The scabbard was finely engraved. At the presentation, the British officer passed the sword to a Russian officer, who in turn presented it to Marshal Stalin. Stalin tilted the scabbard to examine it, and the sword slid silently out and clattered to the floor, making its first public appearance. The Russian officer swiftly retrieved it and replaced it in its scabbard. Stalin made a gracious speech of acceptance which was translated into English by his interpreter, V.N. Pavlov.

President Roosevelt asked if he could examine the sword and it was brought to him. He drew it out of its scabbard and examined the etched inscription and the design on the blade.

During the ceremony, I shot 250 feet of film and took five photographs.

At 11:30 the next day, Mike Reilly told me the Shah of Iran would be meeting with President Roosevelt at noon at the Russian embassy. The other photographers were alerted as well.

I was called in at 12:10 and I took three pictures of the Shah—two of them with the president and the third of the Shah greeting Elliott Roosevelt. The Shah was a handsome young man, probably no more than two or three years older than I. He was dressed in a military uniform. I also took two pictures of the Shah and Churchill.

Tommy Thompson met me in the lobby and extended an invitation from Prime Minister Churchill to attend his 69th birthday dinner that evening at 8:15.

After lunch, Roosevelt, Churchill and Stalin, with their respective military and diplomatic advisors, met for the first time in plenary session. I was told there would be no photographs.

With the afternoon free, I went into downtown Teheran with some of the Secret Service men to do some shopping but prices were so high that buying anything I could want was out of the question. Yet, shops were filled with goods unavailable in Europe. Wartime rationing apparently had not affected Iran.

In an automobile showroom I saw a relatively new Buick for sale for $45,000. A 1936 Chevrolet had a price tag of $20,000. An automobile tire cost $2,000. A fountain pen, which might cost $5 in New York, cost $20 in Teheran.

I was told that many items in shops were booty stolen by bandits who murdered unfortunate travellers crossing the desert, depriving them of their worldly goods.

As I was looking in a shop window, the proprietor came out and offered me $750 for my Omega chronometer—ten times what I

The Shah of Iran and President Roosevelt at Teheran on November 30, 1943.

paid for it. I didn't dare bargain with him for fear I would be tempted to part with it.

I returned to the British embassy at eight o'clock. Most of the other guests had already gathered inside. Dad took me to Prime Minister Churchill. I wished him many happy returns of the day and thanked him for including me in this celebration. I said good evening to President Roosevelt, who gave me a dry martini from a shaker he had made up. Then we made the rounds to meet the other guests. I knew most of them and Dad introduced me to those I had never met.

Then Dad took me to meet Marshal Stalin for the first time. Stalin and Soviet Foreign Minister Molotov were standing alone in a corner of the room. His face lit up when my father introduced me and we shook hands. His hand was large, strong and hard, as if he worked in the fields. Then he introduced me to Molotov. A Soviet interpreter, named Valentin Berejkov, appeared at Stalin's side and translated our conversation.

Stalin asked me what I did in the army and I told him that I was a combat cameraman and had just come from the Italian front at Monte Cassino after having filmed the D-Day landings at Salerno.

"It's good to meet a fighting man amongst all these," he said with a sweeping motion of his arm to include all the generals, field marshals, admirals and diplomats in the room.

The list of those attending Churchill's birthday party is worth recording here:

Prime Minister Winston Churchill
President Franklin D. Roosevelt
Marshal Joseph Stalin
Mr. Charles Bohlen (who served as FDR's interpreter)
Admiral Sir Alan Cunningham
Admiral William D. Leahy
Mrs. Sarah Oliver
Admiral Ernest King
Sir Alexander Cadogan
Commander C.R. "Tommy" Thompson
Sgt. Robert Hopkins
Colonel Elliott Roosevelt
Major Randolph Churchill
General George C. Marshall
Sir Charles Portal
Ambassador John Gil Winant
Sir Archibald Clark Kerr
Mr. Harry L. Hopkins
Sir Anthony Eden
Mr. Vyacheslav Molotov
Sir Reader Bullard
Marshal Klementy Voroshilov
Mr. Valentin Berejkov
General Sir Alan Brooke
General Brehon B. Somervell
Mr. John Martin
Mr. Holman
Major John Boettiger
General Sir Hastings Ismay
General H.H. ("Hap") Arnold
Lord Moran
Ambassador Averell Harriman
Field Marshal Sir John Dill
Major A.H. Birse (Interpreter)

Formal portrait of Stalin, Roosevelt and Churchill at Teheran on November 30, 1943, the first encounter of the three Allied leaders together.

We all moved into the dining room and sat down to another one of those really great meals I enjoyed on occasion during the war. As I had not had time for lunch that day, I approached it with enthusiasm. I was only halfway through when the toasts began.

The prime minister proposed the first toast to the good health of his distinguished guests, thanking them for helping to celebrate his 69th birthday. Roosevelt then raised his glass of Russian champagne to wish Churchill great happiness on this day and in the years to come. He went on to speak of their close relationship which had grown out of the trials of war.

When Stalin stood up, he offered a toast to the president and the people of the United States. He said the United States was a country of machines capable of turning out between 8,000 and 10,000 airplanes a month, while the USSR, with all its factories working at capacity, could only produce 3,000 a month. Great Britain, he said, could produce between 2,500 and 3,000 a month.

He went on to give the respective production figures of all three countries for tanks, artillery, ships and other war materials.

I could see Churchill shifting impatiently in his chair as Stalin reeled off these production figures. Finally, unable to contain himself, Churchill interrupted Stalin and proceeded to give Great Britain's production figures, which were appreciably higher, and exceeded Soviet production. Stalin then finished his speech without commenting on Churchill's interruption, saying, "If it had not been for the aid of the United States through Lend-Lease, Russia would lose the war, and would have lost it long ago."

It was heartening to me to hear such laudatory comments from Stalin about Lend-Lease aid, particularly since it was my father who administered this huge program. But it was my impression that Stalin was deliberately trying to provoke Churchill, possibly to obtain Great Britain's true production figures or possibly out of sheer mischief.

Later, in the course of the innumerable toasts, my reaction was reinforced when Stalin turned unexpectedly on Sir Alan Brooke, who was seated across the table from him, and accused him of being unfriendly toward the Red Army. Sir Alan Brooke seemed stunned at this verbal jab. He stood up in the silence that followed and seemed at a loss for words. He said that Stalin had misinterpreted what were in fact Brooke's real feelings of true friendship toward the Red Army and all its members. He equated Stalin's misinterpretation of the feelings he had masked to the Soviet use of inflatable tanks and dummy aircraft to mislead the enemy.

At the time, I was baffled by this sharp exchange and could only assume that it related to some tension between the two men which may have evolved during the closed meeting earlier in the day. It suggested to me that Stalin used these sparring tactics to detect sensitivities, strengths and weaknesses of those with whom he was dealing. After dinner, I saw Stalin chatting amiably with Sir Alan Brooke.

The toasts continued in rapid succession as one guest after another rose to toast his opposite number. In the two hours that followed dinner, there must have been 50 or 60 toasts. As each was offered, Stalin got out of his chair, walked around the table to the person being honored, touched glasses, said something complimentary to him, quaffed his glass of champagne, and returned to his place at the table. This revealed a courtesy I did not expect of Stalin. It also demonstrated his large capacity for wine.

At one point, my father remarked that not everyone was emptying his glass of champagne with each toast. I, for one, took only a token sip, but when I stood up to leave the table I had to steady myself.

Dinner broke up at 12:30. Dad and I returned to our quarters where we talked until 2:00 A.M. It was our first opportunity to talk alone for any length of time. He told me what he had done for the war effort: how he was the first American official sent to England during the Blitz; how he brought Russia and the United States closer together when he went to Moscow to meet with Stalin; how he arranged the Atlantic Charter meeting, the Casablanca Conference, and above all, how he engineered this meeting at Teheran with the heads of the three great Allied countries. He also said he thought his "baby," Lend-Lease, had done its bit in winning the war.

There were no pictures to be taken on December 1st, so I rested. That evening, we moved to Camp Amirabar where the U.S. Army Persian Gulf Command under General Donald Connally was assigned to ensure that the supply line of Lend-Lease material to Russia remained open. General Connally had worked with Dad in WPA days.

The following morning, President Roosevelt reviewed the troops at Camp Amirabar. A special wooden ramp had been built overnight so that the president's jeep could be driven up on it for the review. The president made a speech to the troops, revealing to them that he and Prime Minister Churchill had been meeting with Marshal Stalin in Teheran to plan the next phase of the war. He told them he realized that they feel isolated from the war, but he assured them that their task in keeping the flow of war materials to Russia was a vital contribution to winning the war.

After the review of troops, we boarded planes and flew back to Cairo. The Chinese delegation had left Cairo before our return. I had no photo assignments for the day, so I took the film I had shot in Cairo and Teheran to the Army Pictorial Lab in Cairo. I processed the still pictures myself and turned the motion picture film over to the lab technicians to develop and to send back to Washington. I showed President Roosevelt the prints of my photographs and he requested that I make additional copies for Chiang Kai-Shek, Churchill and Stalin, which I did.

The president told me that we would be flying to Malta where he would present the Maltese Scroll to the courageous people of that strategic island for their stanch defense against the fierce and prolonged Nazi aerial assault. He entrusted the beautifully-illuminated scroll to me to copy in black and white and in color. I took care of that assignment the following morning.

Later, I learned that the U.S. Army Chaplains' office in Cairo had arranged a trip to the Holy Land on December 4th, leaving early in the morning by air and returning that same evening. I had no assignments until the next day, so I took advantage of this offer.

On December 5th, I photographed the meeting of Roosevelt and Churchill with Ismet Inonu, the president of Turkey. President Inonu was the only chief of state who accepted President Roosevelt's invitation to occupy the place of honor between President Roosevelt and Prime Minister Churchill.

It was my understanding that at this meeting, Roosevelt pressed Turkey to join the Allies and enter the war against Germany. Churchill, however, promoted Turkey's participation in a British operation against Rhodes. President Inonu was not eager to let Turkey become involved in the war and managed to sidestep the issue.

We flew back to Tunis on December 7th and the following morning I travelled with the president and my father aboard the presidential aircraft, which had been dubbed "The Sacred Cow." Our destination was Valletta, the capital of Malta.

I photographed the president and my father as they worked together on the speech the president was going to give as he presented the scroll "to the people and defenders of Malta."

As we approached Valletta Airfield, the pilot, Major Otis Bryan, came back from the cockpit and informed President Roosevelt that the hydraulic system had failed on the aircraft and that he would have to land without being able to lower the flaps to slow the plane or to brake the wheels to bring it to a stop. He assured the president that he would make the landing safely. The president replied that he had every confidence in his ability to do so. Giving no indication that he was perturbed by this announcement, he and Dad went back to work on his speech.

Major Bryan made a perfect landing but used every foot of that landing strip.

We were driven to the city hall of Valletta, where President Roosevelt delivered his speech and presented the scroll to the British Governor-General of Malta.

The president concluded his remarks by saying he only wished he could stay longer so he could see more of this beautiful island of

Malta. At this point, Major Bryan passed him a note saying the aircraft would not be repaired for another two and a half hours. So the president was able to tour the environs of Valletta by jeep.

The president wanted to see some of our troops who had been in action. His preference was to go to Italy, but the Secret Service and the military authorities deemed that too dangerous, so we went to Sicily instead, where he reviewed the troops.

We flew back to Tunis for an overnight stay. Dad and I went to a highly-recommended restaurant on the outskirts of Tunis for dinner. The restaurant was crowded, but they managed to find a table for us. Soon, word got around that my father was present and we were besieged by people who wanted to shake his hand or get his autograph. Among them was a man who worked for Lend-Lease. He arranged for us to move into a private room where we could eat and talk undisturbed. Together we reviewed all that we had seen and heard during those eventful 21 days.

After dinner we returned to the president's quarters at the "White House." The president and his party, including Dad, were scheduled to fly to Dakar early in the morning to board the USS *Iowa* which was waiting there to carry them back to Washington. When I said goodbye to my father that night, we promised to meet again in Berlin.

On the morning of December 9th, I flew back to Algiers with Major General Smith to begin my long-promised leave.

I had given up my room with the Petit family before I embarked on the landings in Italy, so I found new quarters with a French family named Naberes. I shared these quarters with Staff Sergeant Leonard Cripps who, in civilian life, had been a story editor at Universal Films in California. We became fast friends. He was an accomplished pianist and the Naberes family encouraged him to play for them on their piano. Occasionally he played the pipe organ at a nearby church for weddings.

I met some of the replacements from Astoria passing through Algiers en route for Italy. They sought me out when they learned I had served in Italy, anxious about conditions there.

I told them they would learn, as we did, that the hardest part was living and working unprotected under seemingly impossible conditions: the mud, snow, icy winds, searing heat and extreme fatigue. They would find ways to snatch intervals of sleep among pauses in the roar of artillery fire and the whine of incoming shells or bombs. By being cautions, they would learn how to get close enough to the action to get good pictures without getting killed, although there was always risk involved.

I said it was adrenaline that kept us going, the thrill of knowing that we survived because of our own ability, and the satisfaction of getting the pictures back home so Americans would know what the war was all about.

CHAPTER 10

A FAMILY AT WAR

I was transferred from Algiers to London on January 24, 1944 and assigned to the European Theater of Operations. I was billeted in quarters in Shepherd's Market in the heart of London.

London was being bombed day and night by the Germans. Barrage balloons floated over the city, anchored to the ground by steel cables designed to snare enemy aircraft. Anti-aircraft guns, many of them with women serving as gunners, were stationed in squares and parks. Elderly men and women, recruited as air raid wardens, patrolled the roofs of houses on the lookout for enemy aircraft, pointing out blackout violations, and snuffing out fires as they started. Emergency water supply tanks were positioned on every street to be used to quench fires caused by incendiary bombs. At night, raging fires caused by incendiary bombs burned out of control, casting an eerie flickering red glow on the smoky sky.

By this time, everyone in my immediate family was involved in the war in one capacity or another. My father's role as Lend-Lease Administrator was well known. My mother, Ethel, joined the Red Cross in April 1941 and was assigned to a veterans hospital at Fort Devens. David, my older brother, had joined the navy and was commissioned as a lieutenant JG. He was assigned to the aircraft carrier USS *Essex,* a part of the Pacific Fleet, and was put in charge of a photographic unit on board. Eventually, one of the members of his unit took the photograph of U.S. Marines raising the American flag on Iwo Jima, which served as the model for the famous Iwo Jima statue. Stephen joined the U.S. Marines as soon as he graduated from Hill School.

I had been in London for less than a month when Ambassador Winant invited me for dinner at his apartment. The evening started out pleasantly as we brought one another up to date on our activities since we last met. Then, in the middle of dinner, he said, "Robert, I have some bad news for you. Your brother, Stephen, has just been killed during the assault on the Marshall Islands in the Pacific."

I was aghast, unbelieving. My hands and legs were trembling.

"He died bravely during the second night of the assault," the Ambassador continued. "He and a dozen marines were in hot pursuit of retreating Japanese when a Japanese soldier, who had been passed up as dead, suddenly rolled over with a grenade poised in his hand. Stephen, the only man to spot him in time, quickly shot him through the head, which surely saved the lives of many of his comrades. Stephen was killed by a Japanese rifleman and died instantly. He was buried at sea."

I got up from the table. "I have to go out," I said.

I wandered aimlessly through that war-torn city for three nights and days, oblivious of the bombs, the ack-ack and the devastation around me. All I could think about was that my 18-year-old brother, with whom I had always been so close, was dead. I had thought he was still in basic training.

Finally, I returned to duty. No one asked where I had been. No one chastised me for being absent. Everyone knew my brother had been killed in action.

Dad sent me a cable containing a report by Stephen's commanding officer describing how he died. I wrote to my mother, my older brother and my father, sharing my grief with them. Later, I learned that David was involved in the same action, but each was unaware of the other's presence.

My father also sent me a photocopy of the scroll that Prime Minister Churchill had sent him after Stephen was killed. Written in script on parchment, it read:

Stephen Peter Hopkins
Age 18

Your son, my Lord, has paid a soldier's debt;
He only liv'd but till he was a man;
The which no sooner had his prowess confirmed
In the unshrinking station where he fought,
But like a man he died.

—Shakespeare

To Harry Hopkins from Winston Churchill
13 February 1944

I took my copy of the scroll to 10 Downing Street, where I met with Prime Minister Churchill in the Cabinet Room to thank him personally for his thoughtfulness in sending this apt quotation to my father on the occasion of Stephen's death in action. At my request, he kindly signed it for me.

I threw myself into my new assignment, which was to film the preparations for the Normandy landings. Our three-man team was composed of Sergeants Dick Ham and Bruce Bacon. The juxtaposition of the last names of these two soldiers caused considerable amusement whenever we checked into hotels for lodging.

We ranged all over England and Wales, recording on film the stockpiling of tanks, artillery, and landing craft. Epping Forest concealed such massive quantities of tanks, trucks, and heavy artillery that it seemed as if the island would sink under the weight of all this war material.

There were no road signs to guide us as we travelled about. They had all been taken down or obliterated as a measure of security in the event the Germans attacked England. Even though we had maps, we frequently got lost. When we stopped to ask directions of the local inhabitants, they became suspicious of us and declined to help. They had been trained to assume that anyone asking directions could be an enemy.

We were back in London to replenish our stock of film a month after I learned that Stephen was killed. As a change of pace, I went to a dance at the Washington Club on Curzon Street. Here I met Brenda Stephenson, a girl of 18, breathtakingly beautiful, with long dark hair and blue eyes. The despair that had gripped my heart at the loss of Stephen eased off as I held her in my arms and we danced together. I sensed that a miracle had occurred which would change my life.

In the days which followed, Brenda and I spent every free moment together and I learned something of her life as a child in Lancashire and her ordeal during the incessant bombing of London over the years. She had courage and compassion as she faced the terrible and wanton destruction around her every day and night. Yet she retained the gift of laughter and the ability to treasure every moment of life. She was constantly in my thoughts when I returned to my film assignment, and I wrote to her every night.

On May 27th, I was back in London with the film completed. As soon as I could get away from the office, I went to see Brenda. I knew I would be sent to France soon, so that evening I asked her to marry me and she accepted. I then told her parents. I wanted them to know my true intentions about marrying Brenda. They were not thrilled at the prospect, realizing that Brenda would be leaving them after the war to be with me in America.

The following evening, to celebrate our engagement, I took Brenda to the Savoy Hotel for dinner. As we walked through the lounge, Randolph Churchill hailed me. He was seated at a table with four attractive young women. I introduced Brenda to him and he asked us to join them for a drink. I thanked him, but declined. This was a special evening that I didn't want to share with Randolph, who seemed eager to add Brenda to his collection.

The next day, I started the paperwork with the U.S. Army for permission to marry Brenda.

Prime Minister Churchill again invited me to spend the weekend with him and Mrs. Churchill at Chequers the following Saturday. This time, the guests included Lord Cherwell, who was Churchill's scientific advisor; Brendan Bracken; Randolph, and Tommy Thompson, who drove me out there.

Lord Cherwell brought with him some photographs to show to Churchill. After the prime minister examined them, he asked me to look at them. He explained to Lord Cherwell that I was a U.S. Army photographer and the pictures would be of interest to me.

The photographs showed four British soldiers sitting on the grass playing cards. The picture seemed to have been shot from above. Lord Cherwell explained that the photos had been taken at night from an aircraft flying at an altitude of 7,000 feet. This seemed incredible because the cards each man was holding could easily be read and I could see which had the best hand. Evidently, the British had invented a new lens and an extremely sensitive film to be capable of this feat. I told Lord Cherwell that this was a remarkable and valuable achievement.

At dinner, Randolph, who had consumed a few drinks ahead of time, began speaking in a loud voice, effectively silencing others at the table. His father admonished him severely, ordering him to be silent and to speak only when spoken to.

Randolph's wife, Pamela, arrived the following morning with her 18-month-old son, Winston, a miniature replica of his grandfather. This was the only time I saw Randolph and Pamela together.

Before leaving, I told the prime minister I had been filming the impressive preparations for the Normandy landings and expressed the hope that I would be there to film the invasion itself. I thanked him and Mrs. Churchill for their kindness and their friendship. Tommy Thompson gave me a lift back to London with him.

A few days later, all the photographers and cameramen were called into a meeting by our commanding officer. He asked for volunteers to take part in the D-Day landings in Normandy. Assuming there would be plenty of volunteers, I immediately raised my hand, and was shocked to realize that I was the only one who did.

In the discussion that followed, the other men gave various reasons why they felt they should not take part in the first wave. Our commanding officer listened but made no commitment to me or to them about our assignments.

Later I talked to Commander Harry Butcher and told him I was eager to go into France early, either with the paratroopers or the gliders. He strongly urged me not to take part with the paratroopers, saying he had jumped one as part of his training and he made a very hard landing. He reminded me that I had sprained my ankle going over an obstacle course in Oran, which took me out of the assault on Sicily. He suggested that the gliders might be a less hazardous choice. Accordingly, I applied to be attached to the gliders.

Rumors began circulating that I would not be in the first wave, or even the second and that it could be a week or two after D-Day that I would land in France. Disturbed at this, I wrote to my father expressing my desire to be there on D-Day.

It wasn't until after the war was over that I learned that he wrote the following letter to General Eisenhower on May 3, 1944, which is preserved among the Eisenhower Presidential Papers in the Eisenhower Library in Abilene, Kansas:

Dear Ike,

....I hope you will let Robert go on the invasion whenever it comes off. I am fearful—and I am sure Robert is too—that because one of my other boys had some bad luck in the Pacific that Robert's C.O. may be a little hesitant about putting him in. The war is "for keeps" and I want so much to have all of my boys where the going is rough.

General Eisenhower replied in a three-page hand-written letter.

Secret

Supreme Headquarters
ALLIED EXPEDITIONARY FORCE
Office of the Supreme Commander

May 20

Dear Harry,

My first reaction upon receipt of your letter was one of delight that you had sufficiently recovered your strength to write a note. Then, as I read your letter carefully, I began to realize what it must have cost you to insist that Robert's post of duty be one that brings to him a full share of the risks of battle. Your letter is unique among the many hundreds I have received, and, even at the risk of appearing a bit sentimental, I simply must say that I admire and salute your attitude.

Actually, what I shall do is this: I will see to it that no special arrangement or plan of operation in the Photo Service is set up to keep Robert out of the worst spots. On the other hand, I think it would be unwise to step in and direct that regardless of other arrangements already made on the basis of best utilization of personnel, he is to accompany an assault wave. He will be treated as a soldier, on a strictly official basis. Nothing more; nothing less.

I am delighted you are to go to White Sulphur. It is a fine spot.

My very best wishes to you for a complete recovery and, as always, warm personal regards.

Cordially,
Ike

Before long, men began leaving our outfit for embarkation ports in preparation for the landings in France. Torn between my desire to be with Brenda and my determination to take part in the landings, I waited with anticipation for my orders to come through. Still they did not come. Soon there was just a skeleton staff left in London and we were assigned to scrubbing out our billets prior to returning the building to its owners. We were on our knees at that task on June 6th, when the invasion began.

On the night of June 12th, we experienced the first wave of "buzz-bombs" on London. These were German V-1 unmanned flying bombs, the size of a small airplane, stuffed with high explosives. We could see them flying low over the city, illuminated by searchlights. Tracer bullets from anti-aircraft guns arched toward them, but they flew on, powered by a rocket engine. Suddenly, the engine stopped on one of them, and we rejoiced that it had been shot down. Our elation lasted only the 30 seconds it took for the V-1 to fall to the ground with a tremendous explosion. Others followed, indiscriminately demolishing homes, offices, schools, factories, hotels, churches and theaters. This was the beginning of a new kind of warfare calculated to destroy the city and break the spirit of Londoners. Certainly they created havoc, but they only hardened British determination to survive and prevail.

CHAPTER 11

NORMANDY AND BEYOND

Finally, my orders came through to report to the embarkation center at Portsmouth. Our two photography teams consisted of Sergeants Knight Harris and Bruce Bacon; Corporal Ernest Reshovsky and me; plus two drivers—Privates John Smith and John Simms. We were under the command of Lieutenant Marquant.

Harris, a technical sergeant, was a combat cameraman and his partner, Bacon, was a still photographer who had worked for the *Washington Star* before the war. Reshovsky was my partner. He was a Czech who escaped from Europe when Paris fell to the Germans. He got to America and joined the U.S. Army Signal Corps as a still photographer. Simms was a big-boned American of Polish extraction. He was married and had two children. Smith was an American Indian of the Chemiwevi tribe in California. His unfailing good humor kept our morale up in the months that followed.

In Portsmouth, in preparation for the assault on France, we waterproofed our vehicles, a weapons carrier and two jeeps. We were assigned to an LST landing craft with our vehicles.

Violent storms over the English Channel delayed our departure for France for several days. When we finally left, we were a part of a flotilla of hundreds of landing craft and warships. Streams of Allied aircraft streaked over our heads toward France. We didn't experience any enemy action on the way across the Channel, but were subjected to artillery fire from the Germans when we landed on Utah Beach, between the towns of Carentan and Ste. Mere Eglise.

Our troops had gained control of a road about five miles inland by the time we arrived. Beyond that line, the Germans were deeply entrenched behind thorny hedgerows that were virtually impenetrable. Cherbourg was still in enemy hands and the British forces had not yet succeeded in capturing Caen.

St. Lo was one of the landing points of the glider assault and it was fortunate for me that I was not a part of that operation. I was told that our troops suffered terrible losses because in the pre-dawn hours of D-Day the lead aircraft dropped a flare path in the wrong location, marking the landing site in the midst of a heavy concentration of German forces which decimated our men as they scrambled to get out of their gliders.

I prevailed on the pilot of a Piper Cub reconnaissance plane to fly me over Cherbourg so I could film whatever action I could discern. It was my first flight on this kind of aircraft and I felt particularly vulnerable. It seemed flimsy indeed with its canvas skin and the hinged window which dropped open when I released the catch to begin filming. As we swooped down over the jetty protecting the port, German soldiers emerged from a building at the end, waving white flags of surrender. The pilot and I, of course, were in no position to capture them but I reported this to an infantry officer after we landed back in territory we controlled near Ste. Mere Eglise, leaving it to him and other elements of the VII Corps to make the capture.

On the outskirts of Ste. Mere Eglise, we encountered a group of the *Maquis*, members of the French resistance movement who had remained in France, harassing German troops and sabotaging their installations during the German occupation. They told me of the hardship they had endured and their elation that we had finally landed in France. One of them told me that something strange was going on at Bricquebec, a village located between Valognes and Carteret. He said that all the inhabitants had been herded out of the village, which was sealed off by the Germans.

Reshovsky and I decided to investigate. Bricquebec had just been captured and our troops were in the process of consolidating their position. Just outside the village limits, was a huge construction site. It was concealed by camouflage netting and the mountains of earth which had been bulldozed were painted with wavy stripes of black paint to camouflage the purpose of the site. A railway track had been laid and a locomotive was hidden under the netting. Most important, and disturbing to me, was a massive, sloping concrete ramp that appeared to me to be a launching site for a long-range missile. I filmed the installation from every angle, and using my range-finder, measured its length, breadth and thickness, as well as

Robert Hopkins at the Liberation of Cherbourg on June 30, 1944.

the degree of its incline. I turned over all the information I had gathered to army intelligence. It seemed likely to me that this was a launch site for the pilotless V1 flying bombs which were causing such devastating damage to London.

We lunched with our troops who had occupied the village. They had hired women they found there, none of whom spoke French or English, to work in the kitchen. I learned they were slave laborers from Latvia and Estonia, pressed into service by the Germans.

Back in Carenton, a town which I thought we controlled, shots were fired which seemed to come from the steeple of the stone church in the center of town. There, a sniper was concealed and was firing at random at U.S. soldiers. My companions rushed out with their rifles cocked and took positions around the church. I was armed only with a Colt .45 revolver, hardly an adequate weapon for this situation. I filmed the siege, which lasted about 30 minutes. The sniper was finally killed and his body was brought down to the square. He was clad in civilian clothes.

Reshovsky, Simms and I ranged over much of the Cherbourg Peninsula, filming and photographing the various aspects of the campaign. During the liberation of Cherbourg, we moved in and recorded on film the fierce house-to-house fighting.

I encountered Commander Butcher in the port area of Cherbourg. He seemed glad to see me and took a photograph of me that he said he would send to me and to my father. After the war, I found the picture among my father's papers. On it, Commander Butcher had written:

Dear Harry,

I took this snap of Robert in Cherbourg, May 30, 1944. He was griping because he was not in a combat unit. But he had just flown over the outer port, which had just surrendered, to make some pictures. He's very much in love too.

Best wishes and good luck.

Butch SHAEF May 30, '44

Commander Butcher's note suggests that I was in Cherbourg a week *before* the Normandy invasion. In fact, he took the picture on June 30th.

On July 1st, after the city was secured, we took over a house high above the port and established it as our headquarters. In the garage, we discovered a grisly reminder—a German helmet with a bullet hole in it—of the former occupants. It was evident that the German soldier was wearing it when he was killed. There was also a mangy dog, which John Simms adopted as our mascot.

I talked with many French people as I covered various aspects of our presence in Normandy and I obtained a fairly clear idea of what they were thinking and feeling.

Robert Hopkins with members of the Maquis in Normandy.

By and large, they were happy to see us and to be out from under the Nazi yoke. But in towns we had recently liberated and which had received a heavy pounding from our bombs and artillery, many were dazed and distraught. Often, members of their families had been killed and their homes destroyed. Understandably, they did not receive our forces with open arms—not at first. Later, when the shock wore off and they realized that the Germans had been routed from their sector, they warmed up to us.

They told me that during the two months immediately before our landings there, the Germans seized the finest homes for their living quarters, forcing the owners into the street to fend for themselves. After the liberation the owners were able to return and they found their homes in a filthy state with their furnishings broken and tattered. Cartridges, old letters, dirty laundry, cheap French novels, and empty wine bottles littered the floor, tables and beds, providing an insight as to how the "master race" lived. They showed me some of these houses and I could confirm what they told me.

On July 6th, I wrote to my father about this and about their attitude concerning the future of France:

Robert Hopkins with Robert Patterson, Under Secretary of War, General Eisenhower, and Lt. General Somervell in Normandy on August 21, 1944.

> *They want desperately to work with us because they feel that now is the chance to prove themselves at last. They don't say a great deal about politics for fear they will say the wrong thing. But this seems to be their attitude: They have no use for Petain, but they say, "Because he is old, we must respect him." They are suspicious of Giraud because they feel he must be working with the Germans in order to have made his miraculous escape to North Africa. They look to de Gaulle as their leader because he has always been associated with the Free French. They feel that he, of all the possibilities, has the future and well-being of France in mind, rather than his own personal gains. They said, "We want to help, but the U.S. and England refuse to recognize the man we look upon to be our leader. Are we to be subjected to a puppet as we were during the German occupation?"*

The celebration of Bastille Day, France's national holiday, had been prohibited during the four years of the harsh German occupation. As July 14th approached, General Bradley, the American military commander of the liberated portion of Normandy, proclaimed that Bastille Day would be celebrated again.

I was in the town where the largest celebration was planned and I filmed the preparations and the celebration which followed.

A speakers' platform was erected in the square in front of the town hall while a local brass band rehearsed. Villagers decorated the square and the speakers' platform with French flags and bunting. The U.S. Army provided American flags, a public address system, and a U.S. Army band for the festivities.

At noon, preceded by a fanfare from the local brass band, General de Gaulle appeared and made a speech for the enthusiastic crowd which had gathered. This was followed by a vigorous rendition of "La Marseillaise" by the band. After General de Gaulle left to attend ceremonies in other liberated towns in Normandy, the crowd gathered to hear a concert by the U.S. Army band, which first played marches and then changed to dance music. The French obviously enjoyed both but were reluctant to dance because the Germans never permitted that.

I could see they wanted to, so I got up on the platform and broke the ice by saying this was their celebration and the music was for their enjoyment and entertainment, so if they felt like dancing they were welcome to do so, and there were plenty of American soldiers eager to dance with them. Then I told the American soldiers in English what I had told the French. Despite the lack of a common language, the GIs immediately responded by inviting the nearest French girl to dance. Before I knew it, everyone was dancing. The cobblestone paving was not ideal for this, but no one seemed to mind. Some of the women's dancing was a little rusty because they hadn't danced in years, and the teenage girls had never danced to swing music. But before very long, some of the girls were jitter-bugging with the men.

When it began to get dark, the army band stopped playing, but the French were in no mood to quit. This was their day. They formed a human chain and danced around the Place de la Republique. Then, to the music from the brass band, they danced lively Norman folk dances. They sang all the songs the Germans had prohibited since the fall of France. Wine appeared like magic. A scene, locked in my memory, is that of an elderly woman with tears streaming down her cheeks as she listened to the songs she hadn't heard for so long.

There was a commotion at one corner of the square and I heard a woman scream. I went over to investigate and found that two men had pinned a woman's arms behind her back while a third cut off all her hair because she slept with a German officer. There was nothing I could do, but I could not help but wonder how many Frenchmen in the town had collaborated with the Germans during those years when they thought the Nazis would be in control of France forever.

On July 20th, from our vantage point high above the city, I spotted a convoy traveling at high speed along the coastal road toward the airport. Sensing a story, Reshovsky and I, with our driver, Simms, piled into our jeep and managed to catch up with the convoy. A plane had just landed at Ste. Mere Eglise, six miles from Cherbourg. Winston Churchill, accompanied by Lt. General Lee, emerged from the C-47 with members of his military staff, including General Sir Hastings Ismay and Commander "Tommy" Thompson.

I began filming the prime minister as he emerged from the plane and was greeted by Admiral Wilks, Major General Moore, and Brigadier General Plank. Then he came over to me and grasped my hand, saying, "I see that you made the landings as you hoped you would." He told me he had come to Normandy to inspect the German submarine pens at Cherbourg and launching sites for the V-1 flying bombs which had rained down on London from Kirkville, just outside Cherbourg. He entered one of the command cars in the convoy lined up by the tarmac while "Tommy" Thompson greeted me warmly, as did General Ismay.

Reshovsky and I attached ourselves to their convoy and covered the prime minister's inspection of the Port of Cherbourg which was being reconstructed, and the submarine pens, which had been demolished by the Germans just before the American troops entered Cherbourg.

The convoy stopped briefly in the center of the city and Churchill's car was immediately surrounded by French civilians. They all tried to shake his hand or just touch him. One even lit his cigar. Churchill shouted *"Vive la France!"* and the French responded, *"Vive la France! Vive l'Angleterre!"*

The convoy then moved on to the rocket launching area, where the workings of the rockets were explained to the prime minister. He examined the entire base and bade farewell to his hosts, then climbed into the car to start for his trip back to England. Because of the news value of the story, we rushed the film back to our headquarters in London.

Troops and war materials continued to pour into the rather limited territory we controlled on the Normandy beachhead, facilitated by the steel "Mulberry" artificial harbors which the British had invented, built and towed across the English Channel. These made it possible for ships to unload troops, tanks and other war materials onto these steel piers and from there onto the beaches. Because of our huge concentration of men and materials, our breakout from Normandy was inevitable. I put in a bid to cover the breakout whenever it occurred.

General Eisenhower arrived in Isigny to inspect the situation in Normandy and the progress our troops had made since D-Day. He was accompanied by General Breton Somervell and Under-Secretary of War Robert Patterson. They met in a camouflaged tent which served as General Bradley's field headquarters. I had an opportunity to chat with them briefly while Reshovsky photographed the meeting. Secretary Patterson said he would tell my father that he had seen me in Normandy and would assure him that I was well.

Instead of being attached to General Patton's Third Army, I was ordered to go to the town of Carteret, where the army was making preparations to transform this beach resort into a rest and recreation center for the troops who had been engaged in the landings and subsequent conflicts. My assignment was to film the town as it was before and after the troops arrived.

Carteret was virtually deserted but I found quarters in a chateau. Once installed, I set out to explore the town and its surroundings and film its deserted streets and houses. The beach faced the island of Jersey, which was still occupied by the Germans. I could see German troops on the beach of the island as, I am sure, they could see me. They were isolated there and we were out of rifle range of one another, so they posed no threat.

The army engineers had already cleared the area of mines when I arrived. Most of these were anti-personnel "shoe" mines, small wooden boxes glued together, containing a block of plastic explosive and a detonator. Because they contained no nails, they were almost impossible to detect with electronic metal detectors. There were heaps of these boxes, emptied of their explosives and detonators, all along the beach. I picked up one, took it to my quarters and polished it to a high gloss, using brown shoe polish. I decided to send it to my father as a souvenir of the landings in Normandy.

While working on this assignment, the Third Army, under the command of General Patton, burst out of Normandy, swept across Brittany, skirted Paris and headed northeast toward Germany. The French 2nd Armored Division, attached to General Patton's Third Army, had just liberated Paris when Colonel Popkess, a Signal Corps photo officer with an advance unit, showed up in Carteret with mail from home.

Among the letters for me was a small box containing a diamond engagement ring for Brenda, which I had ordered from my

Uncle Ben, a jeweler in New York. When he saw it, Colonel Popkess said I shouldn't risk mailing such a valuable package to her. Instead, he told me, I should deliver it to Brenda in person. He said that he would cover my absence for three days.

Excited at the prospect of seeing Brenda again, I thanked him, threw some unexposed cans of film into a red and white canvas press bag, and Simms drove me to the airport in Cherbourg. There I met an American major from Public Relations who was carrying wire recordings of the liberation of Paris. To explain my need to get to London, I said that I had film of the Paris liberation and we decided to join forces. He contacted London and arranged to have a jeep meet us when we arrived in England.

The jeep was waiting for us when we landed and we sped toward London, passing right by Perivale, where Brenda lived. I said to the major, "I think I'll get off here."

"No," he replied, "You have important film on the liberation of Paris. You stay with me."

He dropped me off at Grosvenor Square. I decided not to go to our London base on Davies Street because I didn't know how I would be received without written orders. Instead, I went straight back to Brenda's home. She was thrilled by my unexpected return and by the engagement ring which I gave her. The banns had been said at the ancient Perivale Church which Brenda attended and the army had already approved our application for marriage so we immediately began making plans for our wedding, not knowing when I would be back in England again.

We decided the wedding would be a simple one. We talked to Father Hope, the elderly parish priest, and made arrangements with him to get married on August 30th at 5:30 in the afternoon. I was due to return to France the following day. I arranged for Captain George Lollier, a friend from our London base, to be my best man. Then we bought a pair of wedding rings at Bravington's jewelry store in London.

Time was short and clothing rationing was stringent, so a white wedding gown for Brenda was out of the question. She decided to wear a simple dress for the ceremony. I had no choice but to wear my combat uniform, the same one I wore when Commander Butcher took a photograph of me in Cherbourg.

Brenda called her father at work on the morning of August 30th and asked him to leave immediately so he could attend the wedding. Her father, Ben, was an engineer who built hydraulic jacks

Brenda Hopkins shortly after her marriage to Robert Hopkins on August 30, 1944.

for the British navy and could not easily get away from this vital job, but he managed it.

Brenda asked if I wanted to read through the text of the wedding ceremony in advance, but I said I had seen so many wedding scenes in movies that I was sure I knew it by heart—a foolish decision on my part.

We all gathered outside the church. I borrowed a necktie from Captain Lollier's driver and left my steel helmet in his jeep. Then we entered this lovely small church. I gave the rings to Captain Lollier and we took our places.

Father Hope was a very old man and was deeply troubled because his son was missing in action. He kept losing his place and repeating himself. At the point in the service where we took our vows, he turned to me and said, "Repeat after me. I plight thee my troth."

"What did you say?" I asked.

"I plight thee my troth."

I still didn't understand him. "What?"

"I plight thee my troth. Just say it!" he hissed.

So I said it, without having the faintest notion that I had pledged my betrothal to Brenda, the whole purpose of the ceremony.

There was no pealing of the church bell to celebrate our marriage because all church bells in England had been silenced, to be rung only in the event of a German invasion or an eventual Allied victory.

That night, Brenda's parents said they would sleep in the air raid shelter so we could have their house to ourselves.

I was conscious of the fact I would have to return to Normandy in the morning. But a heavy fog settled down over London, grounding all aircraft for three days. We revelled in this stroke of good luck.

But Glenn Miller, the popular band leader who had come to Europe with his band for a USO tour, had a different fate. He persuaded the pilot of a small plane to fly him to France on August 31st despite the fog so he could make arrangements for his tour there. His plane took off and was never seen again.

When the weather cleared, I reluctantly took leave of Brenda and flew back to Cherbourg, warmed and stimulated by the knowledge that I had married the girl I loved and would spend the rest of my life with.

Having completed the first phase of my assignment in Carteret, I took on a series of assignments showing how the rear echelons of the army supported the rapidly advancing Third Army. I spent the next two months filming communications centers, supply depots and other service-of-supply activities while trying desperately to break out of this backwater of the war.

Finally, Reshovsky and I covered the Red Ball Express, a series of convoys traveling in rapid succession twenty-four hours a day, loaded with weapons, munitions, food rations and gasoline for Patton's swiftly advancing troops. This ten-day assignment took us to Paris.

Before leaving Normandy, we stopped off in Isigny so I could say goodbye to an elderly farmer who I had befriended shortly after the landings. When I told him we were moving up the front he gave me a wooden tub containing ten kilos of butter, which he wrapped in wet burlap.

"Keep this out of the sun," he said. "And give it to people in Paris. They haven't seen butter in years. The *Boches* took it all." I thanked him and promised him I would.

As we approached Paris, Reshovsky asked if he could take over the wheel, saying he had driven out of Paris just before the Germans marched in and wanted to drive back in. I gladly exchanged places with him. We reported to Colonel Popkess, who now commanded the 3120th Signal Service Battalion (Photo GHQ), our Paris head-quarters on the Boulevard Suchet.

I was directed to my billet in a magnificent six-floor apartment building near the Place de la Muette. It was built by a dozen wealthy French families, with two apartments to a floor. I was assigned to an apartment on the third floor where I shared a large room with three other members of Photo GHQ. It doubtless had been the living room because it had a fireplace and its floor-to-ceiling French windows overlooked a beautiful garden. The room was unfurnished except for four comfortable beds. There was a closet large enough to accommodate all of our belongings. The apartment had a modern kitchen with a big refrigerator, into which I put the tub of butter until I could decide who I would give it to.

I was pleased to discover that Captain Lollier had arrived from London and was assigned as commander of our company. We had a chance to talk privately and he told me he was sorry he didn't have a chance to see Brenda before he left London.

Then he told me he had recommended me for a direct commission as a 2nd lieutenant. I was stunned by this unexpected news. With some confusion, I thanked him.

I had always been happy as an enlisted man and had not aspired to be an officer. I was a T-4 technical sergeant by this time but I realized that the higher officer's pay would be welcome now that Brenda and I were married.

Captain Lollier urged me to get recommendations from at least two officers who were familiar with my performance in the army.

"How high up should I go for these recommendations?" I asked.

"The higher the better," he replied.

Then, as I was leaving, he said I could take a seven-day leave in Paris.

I collected all the mail delivered in my absence. Among these letters was one from my father suggesting that if and when I get to

Paris, I should look up Marie-Louise Bousquet, who had been a good friend of my stepmother Louise when she was Paris editor of *Harper's Bazaar* before the war. He gave me her address and said that Louise had already written to Marie-Louise about me.

Marie-Louise Bousquet lived in a lovely third floor apartment overlooking Place Palais Bourbon. She was a tiny, spritely woman of about 65 years. She had received the letter Louise wrote about me and greeted me as if I were a long-lost son. She pressed me for details about my life, my father and his wife Louise and my work in the army. She seemed fascinated by all I told her. Before I left her, she told me firmly that I must return on Thursday evening, when she held her weekly *salon*, so I could meet her friends.

I returned to Marie-Louise's apartment that Thursday, struggling up the stairs with the heavy tub of butter still wrapped in burlap. She greeted me with open arms. As I unwrapped the tub of butter, her eyes filled with tears with the realization of the bounty I had brought her.

Her guests were already there, and she announced my arrival to them all. Then she dragged the tub into the middle of the living room where everyone could see it and proclaimed that each of her guests would have a share of the butter.

She introduced me to her friends. They were fashion designers, musicians, painters, playwrights and authors. Among them were "Coco" Chanel; Henri Jenson, the French playwright who wrote *Carnet du Bal*; Georges Auric, the composer and conductor; Salvador Dali, the Spanish painter; and the Countess de Noailles, who was reputed to be the wealthiest woman in Europe.

Marie-Louise insisted that I tell them about myself and my encounters with Roosevelt, Churchill and Stalin and others at the conferences at Casablanca, Cairo and Teheran.

The Countess de Nouilles invited me to a party the following evening at her home in the Place d'Iena. There were about 40 people there. The walls of her home were covered from floor to ceiling and frame to frame with fabulous paintings by Picasso, Dali, Cezanne, Degas, Monet, Gauguin, Sisley, Goya, Rubens and others. Obviously she had brought all of these masterpieces from her chateau in the country and crammed them into her much smaller home in Paris.

I was told that later in the evening, a famous French singer would come from the nightclub where she was performing to entertain us. I pictured a tall willowy blonde. Instead, she turned out to be a tiny woman, 45 or 50 years old, with grey hair cut in a boyish bob. But she had a marvelous deep and passionate voice. Her name was Edith Piaf.

Henri Janson and his wife invited me to dinner at their apartment two days later. To my surprise, Monsieur Janson's mistress was also there. The three of them seemed to be the best of friends.

During that short leave, I was able to glimpse into a cosmopolitan world of which I was only vaguely aware.

To my dismay, instead of being sent on to cover the war, Reshovsky, Simms and I were sent back to Normandy. Major Popkess assured me that replacements would be sent to relieve us. Dispirited, we moved back into the house in Cherbourg which we thought we had left forever. We were the only U.S. Army photo unit still in Normandy.

Our next assignment was to make a documentary film about a remarkable operation to get food to Paris when the city was liberated.

Long before the Normandy landings, Allied military authorities of G-5 (Supply) in London realized the dire need for food among Parisians. Because the Allied landings took place in Normandy, the breadbasket of France, the frontlines cut off such products as milk, butter, cheese, meat and vegetables, staples essential to thousands of Parisians.

It was decided that the French themselves would have to carry the food to Paris in French vehicles, since all military transport was needed to carry munitions and supplies to the front. The British Lend-Leased to the French some American vehicles built in Canada, mostly Chevrolets and Dodges, and provided the drivers with uniforms. Food such as coffee, sugar, flour, salt, chocolate and potatoes was supplied by the United States and England to supplement that available in Normandy. The drivers were composed of members of the French Forces of the Interior (FFI), the *Maquis*, and French volunteers. To the Americans was allotted the job giving these Frenchmen basic training, teaching them the operation and maintenance of the vehicles, and providing liaison among the French, English and American G-5 sections. The French provided their own officers and non-commissioned officers to take care of administration of their organizations.

Thirty-five hundred French civilians were involved in transporting the food to Paris. They were broken down into three regiments and 33 companies, with 50 vehicles to a company. Approximately five convoys of 50 trucks each travelled to Paris every day.

The convoys were run in a triangular rotation system with one convoy en route to Paris, another on the road back, and a third at the base, loaded and ready to leave at as soon as a convoy returned.

In just 18 days, 3,500 French civilians were trained and put in uniform and began delivering food to Paris. In that short period of time, over nine million pounds of food were delivered at a rate of 1.5 to two million pounds a day to alleviate the plight of Parisians.

Our film documented that extraordinary feat.

John Amanitides was sent to us as a replacement for Reshovsky on November 9th. He was described as a veteran still photographer with plenty of professional experience. He had been a cook—and a good one—in the army outfit from which he was transferred to us and we benefited from his considerable culinary talents. He was happy to be with us and was a welcome addition to our small unit. I assigned him to work with Reshovsky. A motion picture cameraman named Phil Schintz arrived the following day. He would take my place.

To break them in, I had them accompany us to film and photograph the various memorial ceremonies commemorating Armistice Day in Normandy on November 11th.

The most moving of these took place at La Cambe Cemetery, where thousands of American soldiers killed in the Normandy landings were buried. After the speeches by American army officers, the firing of a three-shot salute by an American honor guard and the playing of "Taps," the American officers and men left.

A large crowd of French civilians from surrounding communities remained, standing in the rain. I was moved by the fact that these people, dressed in their finest Sunday clothes, had walked for miles along muddy, convoy-filled roads, to pay homage to the American soldiers who had died for the liberation of France.

A French priest detached himself from the group and addressed them. He said he wanted to assure the Americans present (the five of us) that they would care for the graves of these fallen Americans throughout the years and they would never be forgotten.

Then, five elderly men—mayors from surrounding towns— placed wreaths on the ground under the American flag which was flying at half-mast. They raised their gnarled hands in salute while a French band played the American national anthem and the "Marseillaise."

With the formalities over, the people moved through the cemetery, placing flowers on the graves. There were children, five or six years old, clutching flowers in one hand and holding onto an older person with the other. Most were bewildered, not understanding what was going on. They knew only that it was important and solemn. There were also the elderly who felt the heart-piercing stab of two world wars, their faces creased with painful memories and sorrow. Young people were there as well—nearly all were girls since most of the young men were in the army. They had seen for themselves the terrible cost of war and true meaning of Armistice Day.

I later learned that each family adopted certain graves and cared for them, placing fresh flowers on them every Armistice Day.

We returned to Paris, where our unit was disbanded. Reshovsky and Simms were given other assignments. I took this opportunity to obtain the two letters of recommendation I required for my commission as a Second Lieutenant. I went to the Supreme Headquarters Allied Expeditionary Forces (SHAEF) where General Eisenhower and Lt. General W. Bedell Smith were kind enough to write the letters. General Eisenhower's letter read as follows:

Supreme Headquarters
ALLIED EXPEDITIONARY FORCE
Office of the Supreme Commander

November 1944

TO WHOM IT MAY CONCERN:

I have known S/Sgt. Robert Hopkins of the U.S. Army Signal Corps for almost two years. I have noted that he is devoted to his duty, which is that of a Signal Corps photographer, and is tireless in its performance. In numerous contacts with him he has always impressed me as being an excellent soldier.

(Signed)
DWIGHT D. EISENHOWER
General, U.S. Army

For his part, General Smith wrote a letter in these terms:

Supreme Headquarters
ALLIED EXPEDITIONARY FORCE
Office of the Chief of Staff

21 November 1944

TO WHOM IT MAY CONCERN:

I have known T/Sgt. Robert NMI Hopkins, Serial No. 32183182, for some time. I consider him to be trustworthy, thoroughly reliable and highly intelligent, and I believe that he possesses the qualifications necessary to perform the duties of an officer in his particular specialty.

(Signed)
W.B. Smith
Lt. General, U.S.A. Chief of Staff

I submitted these letters with other documents required for the appointment.

In the latter part of December, I was sent to England on temporary duty for seven days and was reunited with Brenda for the first time since our wedding.

Lord Beaverbrook, whom we had come to know during our courtship, invited us to spend Christmas weekend with him in his country home, an enormous, rambling mansion near Leatherhead called "Cherkley." He had been more than kind to us since we first met and had become our champion by writing glowing letters of praise about Brenda and me to my father at a time when my father had some reservations about our plans to get married.

He was a Canadian named Max Aitken when he went to England and established himself as an influential newspaperman by publishing two major London newspapers, *The Daily Express* and *The Evening Standard*. He was raised to the peerage and took the name Lord Beaverbrook. He held an important position in the Churchill cabinet as Lord Privy Seal.

As in the past, he sent his Rolls-Royce to meet us at Leatherhead railway station. Other guests were already present when we arrived: his granddaughter, Jean Aitken; Pamela Churchill and her four-year-old son, Winston, who was speeding around the ground floor in a kiddy car that Lord Beaverbrook had given him for Christmas; Lord Forbes, a cousin of the queen; and the Norton identical twins, two attractive and vivacious young women.

Lord Beaverbrook took us on a walking tour of the extensive grounds surrounding his home. His Rolls-Royce followed us down the hill discreetly and as we turned back toward the house, Lord Beaverbrook, in a concession to his age, got into it so he would not have to climb back up the hill.

At intervals, while we were having cocktails before the midday meal, Lord Beaverbrook would suddenly shout for his secretary, Kneuckles (pronounced "Knuckles"), to dictate a memo or message that came to his mind. Then his secretary would retreat and disappear, only to be called back a short time later to take more dictation. Even in relaxed social circumstances such as this, Lord Beaverbrook never stopped working. I always thought that "Knuckles" was an inappropriate name for this timid, but efficient, young man.

As we were about to sit down to Christmas dinner, Ambassador Gusov, the Soviet emissary to England, arrived unexpectedly. Lord Beaverbrook offered him a drink and proposed a toast to the valiant Red Army. Ambassador Gusov responded simply by saying "*Da.*" He did not return the compliment by offering a toast to the British Armed Forces which had stood alone against the Nazis for years before the Russians became involved in the war. The two men talked privately, then the Ambassador left before dinner.

Christmas dinner was a multi-course affair accompanied by a fine wine from his cellar. I was woefully ignorant about wine, and when I said nothing about its quality he said, "If you don't say something about this wine, I won't fill your glass again!"

Our weekend there was a memorable one and we were fortunate to be invited back repeatedly whenever I was in England. I returned to Paris on December 31st, grateful for having had the opportunity to be with Brenda again.

On January 4, 1945 I received orders to proceed immediately to a combat zone in Germany under the command of Lieutenant Oakes. My orders read that the assignment was "not to exceed seven days."

Our unit consisted of two camera teams. My teammate was Arthur Gaush, a still photographer who had no combat experience although he had come over with me aboard the *Dempo* in 1942. He was engaged to a girl he met in Liverpool and had planned to marry her a week after he received orders for this assignment. Sgt. Bobby Quirk, a movie cameraman who had seen plenty of action, and Sgt. Joe Lovell, a still photographer who had earned the Distinguished Service

Cross, made up the second team. A driver, James Quinn, who had seen a good deal of combat in Normandy, completed the unit.

We left Paris in three jeeps in a blinding snowstorm, heading northeast through Luxembourg and into Germany, crossing the Rhine River at Cologne. It took us days to reach our destination. I have never been so cold as I was in that trip to Germany, exposed as we were in those open jeeps. Freezing winds swept across the plains and pasture lands, blowing the snow into drifts as high as the roof of our jeep, frequently concealing the road entirely. Our olive-drab vehicles stood out in stark contrast to the snow, making us easy targets. Fortunately, the army had set up mobile "hot chow" units along our route where we could get hot coffee, soup and sandwiches.

At the end of our first day of traveling, Lieutenant Oakes found us a place to sleep in an abandoned farmhouse. There was ample firewood and we immediately built a roaring fire in the hearth. As we warmed ourselves, Lieutenant Oakes briefed us on our mission.

He assured us that he would always endeavor to find us shelter such as this so we would not have to dig foxholes in the frozen earth and sleep exposed to the elements. Then he told us the sobering news that although our orders read for only seven days, we must expect to stay for weeks or even months on this assignment. This, he said, was the beginning of the last phase of the war as our troops surged toward Berlin. Using a map, he showed us the sector in which we would be operating and the army units we were to cover in action.

The next morning, before we left the farmhouse for our long trip to the front, we found a container of whitewash in one of the sheds which we used to paint our jeeps and our helmets. We completed our camouflage by draping ourselves in sheets we found in the farmhouse.

When we reached our destination, we reported to Major General Harry J. Maloney, commander of the 94th Infantry Division at Ramaling, Germany. When Lieutenant Oakes apprised him of our mission, the general put us in touch with his G-2 officer, who briefed us on the current situation.

He said our forces in this sector were opposed by hard-bitten SS troops who had fought on the Russian front, and two divisions of the Peoples' Army. The latter was composed of elderly men and boys as young as 14—Germany's last human resource. I learned when I got into action that these Germans fought with ferocity born of desperation as we forced them to give up their land little by little.

My caption sheets for that period show that I covered the 94th Infantry Division in action at Ramaling, where I filmed Private 1st

Class Herbert Austin being awarded the Distinguished Service Cross for knocking out a German machinegun nest with his BAR while under fire; the 179th Engineers, who were clearing out mines at Holstaff; the 733rd Field Artillery, XX Corps, where the men were whitewashing the barrels of 155-mm guns between salvos, and covering 50-mm anti-aircraft guns with netting interlaced with white paper; the cooks of the 301st Infantry Battalion setting up a chow line at the edge of the woods near Ritzing so that GIs in nearby foxholes could emerge to get a hot meal; a reconnaissance patrol from the 94th Infantry Division scouting for a machinegun position along the bank of the Moselle River; troops crossing the "Dragon's Teeth" of the Siegfried Line near Tettingen while under incessant fire from German artillery; the fierce fighting at Tettingen, where we held one half of the town and the Germans held the other half; German medics with flags of truce retrieving wounded German soldiers from the battlefield around Tettingen and carrying them back to their own lines; cooks from headquarters company carrying a huge cauldron of hot stew across the Siegfried Line under fire and up the hill to our men on the front line in Tettingen; and the advance of the 302nd Infantry at Perl.

As our base of operations, we took over a building which had just been vacated by the Germans in the part of Tettingen we controlled. The Germans had used it as a mess hall. Before that, it had been a school house. We patched the broken windows with tarpaper, eliminating some of the icy drafts that swept through the building, then went out on a scavenger hunt and found a pot-belly stove, some stovepipe and coal. In no time, we got a fire going in the stove and huddled around it to get warm.

In rummaging around, we found a cardboard box which had contained frozen chickens. There was still one solidly frozen chicken left in it, stuck to the bottom. Although we had never seen frozen chicken before, we boiled it on our stove in a battered pot we found. It was a great improvement over the cold c-rations we had been eating for days.

Because there were no beds, we slept on the long tables which had recently served as mess tables for German soldiers and had once served as desks for school children.

At a quartermaster outfit I visited, I discovered the ingenuity of men there who had devised a heating system far superior to ours. They had taken an empty 50-gallon oil drum, cut it in half around the middle, pierced a row of holes round the bottom above the rim, and filled it with boulders from a nearby stream.

They then inverted the other half of the drum and fixed it to the wall above the lower half. Next, they welded a butterfly switch to a length of quarter-inch metal tubing which they inserted into what had been the top of the drum, with the tubing leading down to just above the boulders in the lower half. Finally, they filled the upper half with used crankcase oil. With a blowtorch, they heated the boulders. When they were very hot, they opened the butterfly switch just enough so that oil dripped onto the hot stones one drop at a time and ignited. They could adjust the intensity of the heat by opening or closing the butterfly switch. The holes around the bottom of the drum provided the draft needed to keep the fire blazing.

Their quarters were the warmest in the sector.

There were signs of inventiveness everywhere I went. At Ritzing, there was a machinegun company composed of men from the hills of Tennessee, who manned their guns in shifts. When they were off-duty, they slept in a nearby barn where they found piles of potatoes and apples abandoned by the farmer. In a matter of days, those who were off-duty constructed a distillery from scraps of metal they found in and around the barn and soon were producing substantial quantities of 90-proof alcohol distilled from the apples and potatoes. They labelled the clear liquid applejack if it was made from apples or vodka if it was made from potatoes. They transformed the vodka into Scotch by tinting it with tea. They soon had a thriving business, selling the stuff to troops nearby. Their primary concern when I left them was that while they produced plenty of liquor, they didn't have enough empty bottles to sell it all.

After three grueling weeks at the front, and a heavy dose of battle, I was suddenly ordered back to Supreme Headquarters in Paris. Quirk and Quinn returned to Paris with me for reassignment.

In Paris, I was issued a Speed Graphic and instructed to obtain enough still and motion picture film to last a month. I was issued orders for a 30-day period which entitled me to travel anywhere. I could only surmise that another Big Three Conference was in the offing.

CHAPTER 12

PRELUDE TO THE YALTA CONFERENCE

My father arrived in London for three days of talks with Winston Churchill at about the same time that I returned to Paris from the German Front. Ambassador Winant reserved a suite for him at Claridge's Hotel, close to the embassy.

I was delighted to learn later that the first thing Dad did was to contact Brenda, inviting her to lunch with him in his suite. Brenda was a little intimidated, but her concern melted away when he embraced her and welcomed her to our family.

He had already ordered lunch, and the waiter arrived with two platters of Whitstable oysters. Brenda was dismayed. She had been a vegetarian all her life, and knew she couldn't eat raw oysters, so Dad ordered a vegetable plate for her. Then he devoured both platters of oysters with obvious relish, saying, "My doctors have forbidden me to eat these, but I can't resist them."

They talked for an hour and a half, getting acquainted with one another. He said he hoped to meet me in Paris and would be glad to carry a letter or anything else she wished to send me. Then, because he had a meeting with Churchill, he excused himself and Brenda returned to her office where she worked as a secretary in the U.S. Army Chaplains' Section.

Just before Dad left London, he invited Brenda to Ambassador Winant's office with her parents so he would have a chance to meet them as well. The Ambassador served drinks to them all—sherry for Brenda and her mother, and Scotch for her father and mine. Brenda gave him a letter for me and a balaclava helmet I had asked her to knit for me to

Averall Harriman's meeting with President Roosevelt at Malta, prior to the Yalta Conference.

ward off the bitter cold in Germany. They had time to talk for just a short time before my father had to dash off to catch his flight to Paris.

I met him when he arrived, and rode with him from the airport to Paris. He told me about his meetings with Brenda and her parents, and gave me her letter and the balaclava helmet. I brought him up to date on my activities in Germany and told him I had been recommended for a direct commission as a second lieutenant based on my performance under fire.

He told me that President Roosevelt would be meeting with Stalin at Yalta, in the Crimea, and that the president expressed the wish that I cover the conference if I were not out on another assignment. I assured him that I was available, having just completed the three-week assignment on the German front. He said we would be flying to Rome and from there to Malta, where the president and the prime minister would rendezvous before they both flew to the Crimea.

I was honored that the president wanted me to cover the conference, and excited at the prospect.

General Charles de Gaulle was not invited to the Yalta Conference, and indeed, was unaware that one was in the offing. He knew that sooner or later one would be held and had instructed his foreign minister, Georges Bidault, to cable the State Department suggesting that de Gaulle attend. There was no reply from the State Department. Roosevelt, Churchill and Stalin were in agreement that de Gaulle should not participate because of France's ignominious collapse when Germany invaded, and its limited part in confronting German forces subsequently.

De Gaulle was furious when he was apprised by reporters that a Big Three Conference was imminent. He considered it an inexcusable affront that he was not informed. When asked if he would attend, he conceded that he had not been invited.

De Gaulle had counted on being able to take part as an equal in the discussions concerning the post-war fate of Germany. Because of this, President Roosevelt sent my father to Paris to smooth his ruffled feathers.

Accompanied by the American ambassador to France, Jefferson Caffrey, Dad met with Bidault for a discussion over lunch.

According to Ambassador Caffrey's report to the secretary of state, Dad told Bidault that he had met with Churchill, Eden and British military leaders in London to discuss the present war situation, and he had come to Paris to discuss these matters with the foreign minister and General de Gaulle. He said he felt that relations between the U.S. and France were not all they should be and it was his ardent desire to contribute something to correct this. He said that President Roosevelt was prepared to invite de Gaulle to meet him the day after the conference ended aboard the cruiser USS *Quincy* at Algiers.

Bidault advised against this, saying that de Gaulle would not want to be associated with decisions made at Yalta that had not included him.

Bidault took this opportunity to outline France's position on post-war control of Germany. He spoke about the elimination of all war industry and the creation of an international body to govern and control the Rhine region, where the southern part would be controlled exclusively by the French, the northern part would be under mixed control and Germany would be reduced to a status making it impossible to wage war again.

That evening, my father, Caffrey and Bidault were invited to dinner by General de Gaulle. In his cable to the secretary of state,

Ambassador Caffrey described this encounter between my father and de Gaulle.

General de Gaulle was in the icy mood I have heard about but never experienced. My father repeated what he had said to Bidault, but General de Gaulle was not very responsive. There was then a frank discussion between them of the history of relations between the United States of America and France from 1940 to date and de Gaulle was not conciliatory. "If you really believe that relations between the United States of America and France are not all they should be, why don't you do something about it?" was de Gaulle's general attitude, especially since no reply had been received to Bidault's suggestion that de Gaulle be invited to the Big Three Conference.

De Gaulle acknowledged that the U.S. had done a lot to help France, but he felt frustrated, believing the U.S. only did so grudgingly and while under pressure.

My father reiterated that it was his full intention to endeavor to do something about eliminating the existing strain, and more than that, to restore the traditional cordial sympathetic relations which have always existed between the two countries. A more detailed account of this meeting between my father and de Gaulle can be found in Jean Lacoutre's 1991 biography *De Gaulle: The Ruler 1945-1970*. It includes quotes from de Gaulle's own memoirs.

That afternoon, Dad met for two hours with the French ministers of finance, economic affairs and internal affairs. They then took him to see the St. Cyr railway marshalling yards just outside Paris, which had been severely bombed by heavy bombers from the 8th Air Force. The yards and workshops had been completely demolished and over 1,000 locomotives were destroyed. The tracks, however, had been repaired enough to permit trains to move over them again.

When he returned to the house, Dad brought the three cabinet ministers with him as well as Ambassador Caffrey. This gave me the opportunity to meet them and hear what they had to say. The conversation centered around the vast destruction of the bridges, highways, power lines and public buildings in France. Much of this destruction had been caused by our 8th and 12th Air Forces. While they acknowledged that this damage severely hampered German efforts to get munitions and supplies to the troops, their implication was that since our bombers demolished them the United States should repair them.

President Roosevelt consulting with Ambassador John Winant, Secretary of State Stettinius and Harry Hopkins aboard the USS Quincy at Malta.

On the morning of January 29th, Dad, Charles ("Chip") Bohlen, Lieutenant Colonel Deering Howe, Lieutenant Colonel Charles Cabell and I flew aboard a converted Flying Fortress to Rome, where we were met by Alexander Kirk who by then was our Ambassador to Italy. Chip Bohlen was the State Department's liaison officer with the White House. He and Dad worked closely together.

Ambassador Kirk took us to his official residence, the Barberini Place, which he described facetiously as his "175-room shack." It had been the Roman residence of the illustrious Florentine Barberini family of which Cardinal Maffeo Barberini was the patriarch. He was elected Pope Urban VIII in the 17th century.

It was a palace of monumental proportions. The great hall was so lofty that, according to Ambassador Kirk, mist rolled in during the evening partially obscuring the frescoes on the vaulted ceiling depicting the history of the Barberini family.

Ambassador Kirk told us that when the artist was commissioned to paint the frescoes, he was told he would be paid four pieces of gold a year, would be provided with all paints and supplies, would be lodged and fed in the palace, and could bring in as many mistresses as he wanted for as long as it took to finish the job. The artist, who recognized a good contract, took eleven years to finish his work.

We were the ambassador's guests for the night in the palace and he arranged a dinner that evening in my father's honor. The army sent some photographers over to take pictures that evening. These were men with whom I had served in North Africa, including Leonard Cripps.

While my father was busy in meeting with Ambassador Kirk and others, I invited Leonard to stay after the other photographers left so we could exchange our experiences over the past year. I decided to skip the huge dinner the ambassador had planned so we could talk quietly. Dad and the ambassador were acres away from us in another wing of the palace.

There was a concert grand piano in the great hall and I led Leonard to it. It was a pleasure to hear him play again and his music filled that vast room. He had been playing for about 45 minutes when, attracted by the music, the ambassador appeared. I introduced him to Leonard and he insisted that we both join him and his other guests for dinner. Leonard was a little uncomfortable because he wasn't dressed for the occasion, but the ambassador assured him it would be all right.

The banquet was a lavish affair. There were about 20 guests including the commanding general of the area, an admiral and other embassy officials.

After dinner, Ambassador Kirk asked Leonard to play for his guests. After he played some classical music, Leonard asked for requests. Dad asked him to play Irving Berlin's "Oh, How I Hate to Get up in the Morning!" after which one of the generals asked for "Marching Through Georgia" and then "The Battle Hymn of the Republic." The performance lasted until 11:30 that night. As Leonard was leaving, the ambassador invited him to come back again at a later date to play for him.

A black limousine pulled up in front of the Barberini Palace at ten o'clock on the morning of January 30th. A white-haired man emerged. It was Myron Taylor, President Roosevelt's personal representative to the Vatican. He had come to take my father to Vatican City for a private audience with Pope Pius XII. Chip Bohlen, Colonels Howe and Cabell and I accompanied my father.

Myron Taylor conducted us to the papal suite, where the Pontiff awaited us. After being greeted by the pope, my father presented me to him and I dropped to my knees in awe. The pope spoke kindly to me in heavily-accented English. He welcomed me to Rome, gave me his blessing and put into my hand a small silken pouch containing a mother-of-pearl rosary with a silver crucifix. He then greeted and blessed the other members of Dad's party.

The pontiff invited my father into his library for a private 20-minute audience. Monsignor Montini, who would later be elected Pope Paul VI, was the only other person present. My father never told me what they discussed, nor have I been able to find a written account of their meeting. I can only surmise that Dad expressed his hopes for the outcome of the forthcoming meeting in Yalta.

On a balcony outside the pontiff's quarters, the Vatican photographer, using an antique camera, took pictures of us all, flanked by helmeted Swiss guards armed with long pikes and dressed in 16th-century-style orange and blue uniforms. Then Myron Taylor took us on a whirlwind tour of the Sistine Chapel, where I hardly had time to absorb the magnificent frescoes by Michelangelo before we moved on to see the enormous and splendid Basilica of St. Peter.

We left Rome and flew to Allied Force Headquarters in Caserta. Lieutenant Commander Howard Bruenn, President Roosevelt's heart specialist, had joined our group by then. We were met by Ed Stettinius. Also on hand to greet my father were his old friends, General Joseph T. McNarney (who had accompanied Dad to Moscow to meet with Stalin in July 1941) and General Ira Eaker. While Dad met with them at Allied Force Headquarters, I took the opportunity to look up Cliff Oliver, the still photographer with whom I had worked during much of the Italian campaign.

That evening, Dad, Secretary Stettinius and I went to Naples where Ambassador Kirk had arranged for us to stay overnight in a lovely villa he owned overlooking the Bay of Naples. Here, huddled around a pot-bellied stove, the only heat in the villa, Dad briefed Stettinius on his meetings with Churchill and de Gaulle. Together they mapped out the U.S. position on the agenda for the Yalta Conference.

We flew to Malta the following day, this time aboard the C-54 aircraft which had been assigned to Secretary Stettinius. We were met by Anthony Eden, who drove us to Valletta Harbor. It was filled with British warships of all descriptions. There had been snow on the ground in Paris the day we left, but here in Malta, it was wonderfully warm and the blue sky was cloudless.

As soon as we arrived, the pace of activities picked up. There was a flurry of meetings of the Combined British and American

Chiefs of Staff and between members of the U.S. State Department and the British Foreign Office.

Churchill arranged for my father to have a cabin aboard the HMS *Sirius*, a British cruiser. Here, on February 1st, there was a constant ebb and flow of visitors through my father's cabin as they consulted with him to hammer out topics to be raised with the Russians at Yalta. Dad had a series of meetings with senior British officials and officers including Anthony Eden, Sir Alexander Cadogan, Admiral Sir Alexander Cunningham, General Sir Alan Brooke, General Sir Hastings ("Pug") Ismay, as well as General George C. Marshall and Admiral Ernest J. King. I photographed them as they boarded to confer with Dad.

Prime Minister Churchill was aboard the cruiser HMS *Orion*, on the other side of the harbor. That afternoon I took pictures of the prime minister with the officers and men of that mighty ship. Churchill was seated on a chair flanked by the captain and officers. The remainder of the ship's company, which seemed to number in the hundreds, was sitting, kneeling, standing or swarming over the gun turrets in the background. After I took the pictures, the prime minister said, "Promise me you will send copies of the pictures to the Admiralty for the captain." I assured him that I would.

We were told that President Roosevelt would arrive in Valletta Harbor on the morning of February 2nd, aboard the USS *Quincy*. I was on board the HMS *Sirius* with Dad, Anthony Eden, Secretary Stettinius, Averell Harriman, Chip Bohlen and Sir Alexander Cadogan. They were scanning the decks of the USS *Quincy* with powerful binoculars, trying to get a glimpse of the president as the huge ship glided into the harbor. Finally, Dad spotted him sitting in a chair next to one of the gun turrets.

Dad, Stettinius, Harriman, Bohlen and I sped over there in a launch as soon as the *Quincy* dropped anchor. Admiral William D. Leahy, General Edwin M. ("Pa") Watson, and Mike Reilly were already there. The president seemed happy to see me. He was wearing a pin-striped suit, and surprisingly, a grey tweed golfing cap to protect his head from the blazing sun. He introduced me to his daughter, Anna Boettiger, a tall, attractive woman whom I had never met before. She bore a striking resemblance to her mother. Later, the prime minister arrived with his daughter, Sarah Oliver, who I was pleased to see again. I took some "family" pictures of Roosevelt, Churchill, Dad, Anna and Sarah. I also photographed the president with Admiral Harold L. ("Betty") Stark. I can't imagine how that

Winston Churchill will the full complement of the HMS Orion in Valletta Harbor, Malta, on February 1, 1945.

craggy admiral got the nickname "Betty" but he didn't seem to mind when he was so addressed by his peers and by the president. Admiral Stark was joined by Admiral William F. ("Bull") Halsey and I photographed them with the president.

The British Governor-General of Malta, who looked startlingly like General de Gaulle, paid a courtesy visit to President Roosevelt aboard the *Quincy*.

Dad told me that we would be taking off to fly to the Crimea that night and to be sure I had all my equipment with me. After supper, I reported to Valletta airport at 7:00 P.M.. The airport was crowded with four-engine transport planes, more than I had ever seen in one place before. I boarded the plane to which I was assigned. Exhausted from the events of the day, I fell asleep almost immediately.

CHAPTER 13

THE YALTA CONFERENCE

W e were flying over the Black Sea when I woke up at seven o'clock on the morning of February 3rd. Mike Reilly, who was flying on the same plane with me, said we would be landing at Saki in the Crimea and would continue by car to Yalta, 90 miles away.

When our plane landed, Soviet Foreign Minister Molotov was there to meet us. He remembered me from the Teheran Conference and greeted me in a friendly fashion. Prime Minister Churchill had already landed. The president and my father arrived a few minutes later aboard The Sacred Cow. Also on the president's plane were Anna, Ed Stettinius, Averell Harriman and his daughter Kathy and General Edwin "Pa" Watson, the president's military aide.

Soviet soldiers in dress uniforms lined both sides of the runway. They snapped to attention as the president's plane landed, and a Russian military band struck up martial music. When the president was installed in a jeep and was talking to my father, I used some of my precious 4" x 5" color film to photograph them. That picture proved to be my favorite photograph of President Roosevelt and my father together.

President Roosevelt reviewed the honor guard with Prime Minister Churchill walking alongside the jeep as he did so. Then we boarded a convoy of cars and set out on the bone-jarring, 90-mile drive to Yalta. It took us five hours to drive over that battle-pitted road through the stark, scorched-earth landscape to reach our destination. The entire route from Saki to Yalta was guarded by Soviet soldiers, most of them women, posted within sight of one

Arrival of Harry Hopkins and Franklin D. Roosevelt at Saki in the Crimea en route to the Yalta Conference on February 3, 1945.

another. That drive to Yalta took almost as much time as our 1,400 mile flight from Malta to Saki.

Camouflage paint dimmed the splendor of Livadia Palace, which loomed out of the trees. The Nazi High Command, which had occupied the palace, vacated it only months before we arrived.

My father went straight to bed to recuperate from that grueling journey. He had a private room near the president's quarters on the main floor of the palace. Anna Boettiger, Admiral Leahy, General Marshall, and Admiral King also had private rooms, but just about everyone else had to share with one or more people. I recall that there were sixteen army colonels jammed, dormitory-style, in one room. By a miracle, I found a tiny room up under the eaves of the palace furnished with a cot, a straight-back chair and a small table. I immediately claimed it, enormously pleased at having found a room to myself. That night, I had no sooner closed my eyes than I became aware that I was in fact sharing my room with a horde of Russian bedbugs, which emerged from under the torn wallpaper in battalions.

Livadia Palace, site of the Yalta Conference on February 4, 1945.

U.S. Navy personnel, responsible for the logistics of the conference, came to my rescue with aerosol insecticides. Russian bedbugs, however, were impervious to the spray and they bedeviled me and everyone else in the palace for the remainder of the conference. Years later, Anna Boettiger told me that Admiral Leahy was convinced that I had brought the bedbugs with me from the German front.

Shortly after we were installed in the palace, we received a mimeographed description of the palace and its surroundings. I do not know who wrote it, nor have I seen another copy other than my own since the conference. The portion concerning the palace is worth reproducing here to set the scene for the conference:

> *Livadia, the former summer palace of Czar Nicholas II, is situated 1 1/2 miles from Yalta. The new, or large palace was finished in 1911. Most of the frescoes, panelling, carved doors, etc., were prepared in St. Petersburg. The palace grounds formerly belonged to Count Potocki who presented them to the Romanov family in the*

19th century. The parks, which stretch down to the sea, contain fifteen miles of alley lined with cypress, cedar, yew and bay trees. There are many rare plants and trees in the parks, brought from all over the world by Count Potocki and the Romanov family during the 19th and early part of the 20th centuries.

The first floor of the palace was used by Nicholas and his son, Alexai, for living quarters. The left wing, facing the sea, contained the Czar's study and bedroom. The president's private dining room was formerly a billiard room. The large conference room was the ballroom-banquet hall. The Czar had many bedrooms on the first floor and was wont to sleep in a different room every night, even at times changing his room during the night for fear of assassination. The sunroom facing the sea was Alexai's library.

The second floor was used principally by the Czarina and her four daughters. General Marshall is occupying the Imperial bedroom and Admiral King the Czarina's boudoir. The private outside staircase is said to have been used by Rasputin. The large rooms on the left wing were used by the Czarevnas (daughters) as classrooms. The second floor conference room was a private reception room of the Czarina. The second floor dining room was a private sitting room used only by the Czar's family.

The architect of the palace, Krasnov, often had to give way to the whims of the Czar to the detriment, so he thought, of the palace. To avenge himself, he used lion head caricatures of the Czar as armrests on the two marble benches outside the main door. The similarity becomes striking when a cap is placed atop the lion's head.

In the afternoon of February 4, 1945, the day after President Roosevelt arrived at Livadia Palace, Marshal Stalin presented himself unannounced. There was no time to alert Prime Minister Churchill, who was at his quarters at the Vorontsov Villa five miles away, or to summon the main body of U.S. Army photographers billeted aboard the USS *Catoctin* which was anchored off Sevastopol, 80 miles away. The *Catoctin* was used as the communications link to Washington and many members of the support staff lived aboard her during the conference. It the first U.S. warship to enter the Black Sea since the Russian Revolution, thus reinforcing the concept of freedom of the seas.

When I received word of Stalin's arrival, I was writing captions in my cubbyhole of a room on the top floor of the palace. I scrambled downstairs with my Speed Graphic in time to photograph the president chatting with Stalin in a small waiting room

Churchill's arrival at Livadia Palace for the first plenary meeting of the Yalta Conference on February 4, 1945.

just off the main entrance hall of the palace. The president and Stalin were seated on a plush couch with an inlaid table in front of them. Stalin's interpreter, Pavlov, sat to one side making notes and translating for both leaders.

The meeting was a cordial one and consisted primarily of Stalin welcoming the president to Yalta and making sure that he was comfortably settled. Since it was about cocktail hour, the president repeated a ritual he regularly performed at the White House, that of making up a pitcher of dry martinis. He apologized as he passed a glass to Stalin, saying that a good martini really should have a twist of lemon.

At six o'clock the following morning, when I came down to the main entrance hall, I was astonished to find just outside the door to the waiting room a huge lemon tree on which I counted 200 lemons. Stalin had ordered it flown from his native Georgia to Yalta so the president could serve a twist of lemons with his martinis.

Dinner at Yalta on February 5, 1945, hosted by President Roosevelt. This photograph was featured by Paris-Press Magazine with the headline, "This chair belongs to de Gaulle."

The first plenary meeting of the Yalta Conference took place on the afternoon of February 4th, shortly after Stalin's courtesy call on Roosevelt.

By this time, the entire American, British and Russian contingents of official photographers had arrived. There were 16 U.S. Army still photographers and motion picture cameramen, two British photographers, and at least 30 Russians. Their number was difficult to determine because they wore civilian clothes and blended in with the Soviet Foreign Ministry delegation. There were no civilian press photographers or cameramen at the Yalta Conference.

The main entrance hall of Livadia Palace was jammed with the three-nation delegations and all the photographers. We were jostled from all sides and taking pictures was difficult. I managed to photograph the arrival of Churchill and of Stalin and their greetings to the other notables present. Outnumbered as we were by Russian photographers, it seemed to me that every time I raised my camera to take a picture, a Russian photographer would pop up in

U.S. Secretary of State Edward Stettinius, Soviet Foreign Minister Molotov, British Foreign Secretary Anthony Eden and their senior aides, Marshal Voroshilov, Ambassador Maisky, Ambassador Harriman, Ambassador Gusov, Ambassador Winant, Sir Alexander Cadogan, Lord Leathers, General Maisky, William Matthews, Wilder Foote and Alger Hiss gather on the balcony of Koreis Villa, the residence of Marshal Stalin during the Yalta Conference, for a Ministerial-level conference on February 5, 1945.

front of me, blocking my view. This became increasingly frustrating when the principals moved into the conference room and took their places around the conference table. The photographers were not allowed in the conference room. The only vantage point was through the double doors, and the photographers became unruly as they shouldered one another out of the way to get their pictures. Something had to be done.

When the doors closed and the principals began their delibera-tions, the American and British photographers all complained that the Russian photographers were running interference, hampering the efforts of the rest of us to photograph the event.

Although I was outranked by almost everyone there, I called a meeting of all the photographers, using a Russian interpreter named "Mike" to translate. Mike had been a student at Columbia University when his father served as the *Tass* correspondent in New York. His English was excellent.

When we were all assembled, I spoke, saying this was doubtless the most historic meeting of the war and it was our responsibility to record it on film for the world to see. Because of the limited space in the conference area and the large number of people involved, getting good coverage was a problem. As we scrambled to take pictures, we found ourselves photographing one another's backs rather than those who were making history. I said that the only solution I could see was to reduce the number of photographers.

After some discussion, it was agreed to reduce the Russian contingent to one still photographer and two motion picture cameramen, provided the U.S. contingent was reduced to the same number.

I specified that there be two motion picture cameramen for each contingent because changing motion picture film in 1945 was a lengthy process which involved putting the entire camera and a fresh roll of film into a light-tight changing bag. The camera operator would then slip his arms into elasticized sleeves and by touch alone would open the camera, remove the exposed film and seal it into a can, then open a fresh can of film, thread it into the camera and close the camera. In this process the cameraman could miss filming something of importance.

The British photographers politely declined a U.S. offer to supply them with a motion picture cameraman to bring their contingent up to strength. I suggested that all photographs and films be pooled so that each country would benefit from the efforts of the others.

To my surprise, everyone agreed and the problem was solved. Because President Roosevelt had specifically asked me to cover the conference, I was the only U.S. still photographer to take pictures of the remainder of the conference.

Initially, President Roosevelt had asked me to take both movie and still photographs, as I had done at the previous conferences at Casablanca, Cairo and Teheran. I relinquished the task of taking movies so that two other U.S. Army cameramen could assume that responsibility.

In fact, at the previous conferences, in addition to my still cameras, I had to juggle two movie cameras—a 35-mm Eyemo camera with which I shot black and white film and a 16-mm Filmo camera with which I filmed in color. I would set up the Eyemo on a tripod, aim it at the principals, wind up the camera and turn it on, locking the switch in the "on" position. Then I would race around filming in color, interrupting only to snap pictures in color with a Contax camera and in both color and black and white with my Speed Graphic. The film sensitivities were all different, so I had to calculate the different exposures and make sure everything was in focus. Then I would hurry back to wind up the Eyemo again. It was a daunting task. Today it would be much simpler with lightweight cameras that automatically set the focus and exposure.

I never saw the pictures the others took at Yalta. For that matter, I did not see a complete set of my own photographs until after the war.

In the course of the conference, President Roosevelt sent the following message to the War Department concerning the disposition of my photographs:

TOP SECRET

WAR DEPARTMENT

OFFICE OF THE CHIEF SIGNAL OFFICER

WASHINGTON, 25, D.C.

TO: Chief, Army Pictorial Service
*   The Pentagon*
*   Washington, D.C.*
Subject: Disposition of ARGONAUT Photographs.

1. Request that pictures taken by T/3 Robert Hopkins, 32183182, be kept separate from others taken at the ARGONAUT Conferences.
2. Three 8 x 10 prints of each picture be sent to the White House in care of Harry Hopkins.
3. No negatives are to be destroyed.
4. Judicious cropping is authorized.
5. No pictures to be released until you are advised.
6. All pictures will be classified TOP SECRET.
7. The above request has been approved by President Roosevelt.

For the Chief Signal Officer, ARGONAUT:
(Signed)
IRA H. GENE,
OIC Photographic Section

Prior to the second plenary meeting, I gave my father a Soviet 10-ruble banknote on which I wrote my name and "Short-Snorter - Yalta - 5 February 1945." I asked him if he could arrange to get

Marshal Stalin and President Roosevelt at an unannounced meeting at Livadia Palace on the afternoon of February 4, 1945.

Roosevelt, Churchill and Stalin to sign it for me as a souvenir of the conference.

I watched him take it into the conference room. President Roosevelt and Prime Minister Churchill signed it without hesitation. Marshal Stalin balked, however, obviously baffled.

Later, my father told me that Roosevelt explained to Stalin that the "Short Snorter Club" had been formed by American pilots who ferried bombers across the Atlantic to England, and that anyone who flew across the Atlantic was eligible to join provided he was brought into the fellowship by two members. Stalin pointed out that he had never flown across the Atlantic Ocean, and therefore was not eligible to be a member. Roosevelt said that he was taking it upon himself to waive that requirement in this instance. After a lengthy pause, and with obvious reluctance, Stalin signed.

That evening, President Roosevelt was the host at a dinner for Churchill and Stalin and their immediate staffs, including my father. When I photographed the guests around the dinner table, one seat at

Harry and Robert Hopkins on the stone balcony of Livadia Palace, with the Black Sea in the background.

the end of the table was empty because Major Birse, Churchill's interpreter, had not yet sat down. This photograph was featured on a full page in *Paris-Match* magazine with the caption "The Empty Chair Was General de Gaulle's," reflecting French bitterness at the exclusion of General de Gaulle from the Yalta deliberations.

There was an abundance of beluga caviar at Livadia Palace. In fact, a heaping saucer of caviar for each person was the first course at breakfast every day, followed by herring, bread, fruit and tea. The menu never varied. I found this breakfast hard to deal with early in the morning. I longed for a breakfast of orange juice, fried eggs, toast

Churchill, Roosevelt and Stalin on February 11, 1945, the final day of the Yalta Conference, prior to their "official pose" for this group photo.

and coffee. I knew that the president's entourage included the Filipino mess boys who regularly staffed the presidential yacht *Potomac.* I discovered they had brought with them enough food to feed the entire U.S. delegation of 258 people. Included among their supplies were cases of fresh eggs.

The mess boys did not have a chance to use their skills and supplies because the Russians insisted on cooking and serving all meals. Two head waiters recruited from the Hotel Metropole in Moscow served all our meals. They were an unsmiling pair who spoke no English. I usually had breakfast with my father in his bedroom because there was really no other time for us to be alone together. He was amused as I vainly tried with gestures and sketches to describe to the waiters the breakfast I really preferred to have. Finally, after several days, they triumphantly brought me a platter of one dozen fried pullet eggs, preceded by a saucer of caviar and followed by herring, bread, fruit, and tea.

Generally, I had lunch and dinner in the second floor dining room with members of the Secret Service and the navy staff responsible for communications and logistics. The meals were copious but the menu, which was the same for both lunch and dinner, never varied for our entire stay at Yalta. As with breakfast, the first course was caviar, followed by roast pheasant, string beans, cabbage and potatoes, with pastry and fruit for dessert, all accompanied by excellent Georgian wine.

My father was weak and bed-ridden for most of the Yalta Conference, but he attended all eight of the meetings at which Roosevelt, Churchill and Stalin were present, seated directly behind the president. Many of the lower echelon meetings were held with him in his bedroom. Here he would advise members of the American delegation on positions to take with their British and Russian counterparts at a ministerial or military level.

There was a meeting of the American, British and Soviet foreign ministers on February 5th at Koreis Villa, Stalin's residence during the Yalta Conference. It was a lovely estate with terraced gardens rich in statuary. Craggy snow-capped mountains formed a dramatic background for it. Although it was modest in comparison to Livadia Palace, it must have been the summer residence of a wealthy member of the nobility before the Russian Revolution.

I photographed Secretary Stettinius, Molotov and Eden on the balcony of the villa. I also took pictures of them with their aides including Marshal Voroshilov, Ambassador Gusov, Averell Harriman, Sir Alexander Cadogan, Lord Leathers, General Maisky, "Doc" Matthews, Wilder Foote and Alger Hiss.

On the few occasions when Dad was up and dressed but not involved in a meeting, I took pictures of him with other members of the U.S. delegation, including Ed Flynn, the Chairman of the Democratic National Committee, who had no role to play at the conference but who the president invited along as a courtesy; with Chip Bohlen; and with Steve Early, the president's press secretary. After I took Steve's picture with Dad, I turned my Speed Graphic over to him so he could photograph my father and me together on the balcony of Livadia Palace, with the Black Sea in the background.

When conferences were in session, I was free to photograph the palace and gardens. On one occasion, Anna Boettiger, Kathy Harriman and I took a walk through the grounds and down into the town of Yalta. We were followed at about 20 paces by a Russian soldier. On our way we encountered a child of about four years old. We stopped to talk to him, with Kathy interpreting. Anna offered him a Hershey bar, which he accepted. At that point the Russian soldier rushed up to us, snatched the candy bar from the child and

Churchill, Roosevelt and Stalin at photo session on the final day of the Yalta Conference.

forced it back into Anna's hand, saying, "Russian children don't need food!" Our protests were to no avail and the frightened child ran back to his house, empty-handed.

Farther along, we found a large billboard covered with a propaganda poster directed against Spain's Franco. On examining it, I realized that it was hand-painted. Apparently, there were no facilities in Yalta for printing posters of this size.

Yalta was a charming town and I could understand why it had been such a popular resort. We entered a church, where a Russian Orthodox Mass was in progress. The church was filled to capacity with very old women and young children. All men and women of military age were in the armed forces. There were no pews or chairs and at prayers, the worshippers prostrated themselves on the smooth stone floor. There was a marvelous choir of strong male voices that thundered through the church. Later I learned that it was composed of men well beyond military age. I had understood that religion was stifled in the Soviet Union. But here, at least, it continued to thrive.

The final plenary session of the Yalta Conference was held on February 11th and Steve Early set up a photo session in the courtyard of the palace that afternoon. The sky was slightly overcast, providing good even light for our pictures.

The courtyard was surrounded on all four sides by an arcade and there was a well in the center. Oriental rugs were spread over what had been gardens and three chairs were placed in front of the well for Roosevelt, Churchill and Stalin.

When the photographers were admitted, President Roosevelt and Marshal Stalin had already been seated. Prime Minister Churchill arrived shortly after wearing a Russian fur hat, to the amusement of both Roosevelt and Stalin. Their military and diplomatic staffs were milling around in the background. Dad was too ill to attend and remained in bed.

I sensed a kind of euphoria among the principals and members of all three delegations for all that was accomplished during the conference. Their faces reflected relief from the strain of negotiations and there was a good deal of laughter and good-natured banter among them.

Of particular importance was agreement on the partition of Germany after its defeat, Stalin's acceptance of free elections in Poland with the participation of Polish exiles in London, Stalin's agreement to join American and British forces in the Far East to defeat Japan, and most of all, the three-power agreement on the terms for the establishment of the United Nations Organization as a means for ensuring world peace.

"How do you want to handle this, Robert?" asked the president.

"First, Mr. President, I'd like to have Mr. Stettinius stand behind you, with Mr. Molotov, behind Marshal Stalin, and Mr. Eden behind Prime Minister Churchill. Then I would like the others who participated in the deliberations to move in so that they will be included in the photographic record of the conference."

The three senior diplomats took their places as I requested, but the others did not move out of the way as I had hoped. It didn't really matter because each individual there made an important contribution to the discussions.

Using my Speed Graphic, I took pictures in both black and white and in color. My stock of color sheet film was diminishing, so I used it judiciously. I also took some color pictures with a Contax camera. With the reduced number of photographers and motion picture cameramen present, the 45-minute photo session was accomplished with appropriate decorum and everyone got good pictures.

Six weeks later, after President Roosevelt died of a cerebral hemorrhage, newspaper and magazine editors thumbed through the pictures I had taken and printed the one or two in which the president looked weary and drawn. They passed over those taken seconds before or after in which he appeared presidential, relaxed and good-humored. This prompted political analysts to surmise that he was so sick at Yalta that he made concessions to Stalin which ill-served the national interests of the United States. Later, some historians stressed the same theme. The president was certainly tired on that last day of the conference, but this was not a precursor to a cerebral hemorrhage, which strikes without warning. From my own observations of the president that day, I can state that he was highly satisfied with the agreements reached at the conference.

As I was taking a picture of Stalin and Molotov under the arcade, Stalin motioned me to approach. He smiled and shook my hand and asked me what I had been doing since we last met. Molotov acted as our interpreter as we talked.

I told him that I had just returned from filming action on the German front.

"What are your plans now?" he asked.

"Well, I want to be the first American photographer in Berlin, but this seems unlikely since your troops are on the outskirts of the city and we're 125 miles away."

"How would you like to be attached to the Red Army?" he said. "Then you could be the first American to film the fall of Berlin."

This proposal took my breath away. Without thinking, I blurted out, "Could you arrange that?" momentarily forgetting that he could arrange anything in the Soviet orbit.

"You take care of it from your end, and I'll take care of it from ours," said Stalin.

I thanked him, shook hands with him and with Molotov, then raced down the corridor of Livadia Palace, encountering General Marshall on the way. I told him of my conversation with Stalin and asked if he could arrange for me to be placed on temporary duty with the Russian army so I could film the fall of Berlin.

"Yes," he replied, "I can arrange that."

Thrilled at the prospect, I hurried to my father's bedroom and related to him my conversations with Stalin and General Marshall.

Harry Hopkins with Secretary Stettinius and his senior aides in the dining care of Stalin's luxurious train, formerly the property of Czar Nicolas II.

"You can't go," he said flatly.

"What do you mean, I can't go? It's all arranged! This will be the biggest story of the war!"

"I mean you can't go. Think about it. If you were attached to the Russian army, they'd never let you near the front. Even if you got to the front, they wouldn't let you take pictures; and if you were clever enough to take pictures, they'd never let them out of the country. You go into Berlin with the American army."

I was dismayed, but there was no persuading him. He was adamant and I had to admit to myself that he knew the Russians better than I.

"What will I tell Marshall? What can I tell Stalin?"

"That's your problem," he said.

Deflated, I visited General Marshall in his room and told him what my father had said and withdrew my request for temporary duty with the Russians.

Then I went to Stalin and told him I could not go, but thanked him for his offer.

Harry Hopkins, exhausted after the strain of the Yalta Conference, aboard Stalin's private train to the airfield at Saki for the return flight to Egypt.

Stalin just shrugged his shoulders.

President Roosevelt and most of the American delegation went to Sevastapol to view the devastation of that city, with Chip Bohlen as interpreter. Dad was too sick to make that trip, so Stalin provided a car and chauffeur to drive us to Simferopol where a private train, which had belonged to Czar Nicholas II, was waiting to carry us to Saki. Ed Stettinius and members of his State Department team, including H. Freeman ("Doc") Matthews, Wilder Foote, and Alger Hiss stayed on in Yalta to assemble the vast amount of documents related to the Yalta agreements.

The train was an old-fashioned wooden affair. It was locked when we arrived and there was no one around with a key. The wind had come up and it was bitterly cold in that exposed place. Finally, someone showed up with a key and unlocked the door to the train for us. As we climbed on board, we were confronted by a Russian solder who was on guard. He didn't speak any English and we spoke no Russian, but he seemed to expect us and let us enter. Using sign language, I told him my father was ill and had to get into bed. He took us to a compartment with a Pullman bunk. Dad undressed and climbed into bed.

"See if you can get us some food," he said.

I went out into the corridor and again began to act out to the soldier our need for food and drink. He seemed to understand.

I returned to the compartment and we waited—and waited.

"I spent all that money on your college education and you don't even speak enough Russian to get us something to eat," Dad said.

But then there was a knock on the door and the soldier entered with two glasses of tea, a plate of black bread and a saucer of sunflower seeds.

I couldn't resist taking a picture of my father with the meager supper the soldier offered us. It wrenched my heart to see how pale and thin he was. The strain of his activities during the two weeks from the time he arrived in England to the end of the Yalta Conference drained him of all his energy and strength.

I went out into the corridor again to explore the rest of the train. Near the end of it, I found a galley stocked from floor to ceiling with food and drink. Here, also, were the two stone-faced headwaiters who had served the banquets at Livadia Palace. I tried to explain to them that we had arrived and we wanted to have dinner. But they didn't speak English either. Acting out my message and pointing to the food and wine in the galley, I held up two fingers to show there were two of us. One of them shook his head and held up eight fingers. I tried insisted there were two of us, but he just shook his head. Puzzled, I returned to our compartment, reporting what I had discovered. Dad was wryly amused at my performance. He drank his tea, then closed his eyes for a nap.

About an hour later, Ed Stettinius arrived with his aides. I woke up Dad, who dressed and came out to meet them. It was then that I realized that with their arrival we numbered eight people and the headwaiters could now serve us dinner.

We found the dining car, which was panelled in precious woods. The dining room table was covered with white linen on which were placed bottles of wine, vodka and whiskey with appropriate glasses. There were also saucers of caviar and white bread. In one corner of the dining car was a console radio, which looked somewhat like a Philco. On the front of it was as large circular dial with a map of the world, suggesting that it was a shortwave radio. I tried to switch it on, but it didn't work.

We all sat down for drinks and caviar. In time, the waiters brought out the "Yalta Special" : roast pheasant, green beans, cabbage, potatoes, and, for dessert, fruit and pastries.

Dad retired early, but this time he was conducted to the Czar's bedroom, which like the dining car was panelled and had a huge royal bed. I retired to the compartment we occupied when we first boarded the train. I fell asleep immediately. When I awoke, the train was in a siding next to the Saki airfield. The president and his entourage arrived soon after, having travelled by car from Sevastapol.

Dad and I were together as we flew back to Egypt, this time landing near Ismailia.

CHAPTER 14

THE THREE KINGS

Toward the end of the photo session on the last day at Yalta, President Roosevelt casually remarked to Churchill that before returning home he was going to meet separately with King Farouk of Egypt, Emperor Haile Selassie of Ethiopia, and King Abdul-Aziz ibn Saud of Saudi Arabia. This was not a last-minute decision on Roosevelt's part. Records show that he sent invitations to the three sovereigns on February 3rd, while he was still in Malta, asking each of them to meet with him aboard the USS *Quincy*, which would be anchored in Great Bitter Lake in the Suez Canal.

Churchill was disturbed and uneasy at not being informed in advance that Roosevelt had planned this side trip to a region that Churchill considered to be in the British zone of influence. He recovered quickly, however, and said that he, too, was going to meet these chiefs of state on his way back to England. At the time he did not press the president for details on what he intended to discuss with these sovereigns because there were too many people around them. He was concerned, nevertheless, that Roosevelt's personal encounter with these leaders would diminish Great Britain's authority in those countries.

Immediately after the photo session, Churchill hurried to my father's room, visibly upset, to determine from him why the president wanted to meet the three sovereigns. My father told him he didn't know, although he did know that Roosevelt intended to talk to King ibn Saud about Palestine as related to the fate of the Jewish survivors of the Holocaust. He said he assumed the meetings with the others were simply a matter of courtesy on the part of the president.

King Farouk of Egypt aboard the USS Quincy for his meeting with President Roosevelt on February 14, 1945.

President Roosevelt had a strong sense of protocol and thought it only proper, whenever possible, to meet the rulers of the region in which he found himself. For example, as we flew over Turkey en route to the Crimea, Roosevelt sent the following radio message to President Ismet Inonu: "The president of the United States sends cordial greetings to the president of Turkey." A year earlier, he had done the same when we flew from Cairo to Teheran, sending similar messages to the rulers of countries over which we flew.

When I remarked to Mike Reilly that this practice seemed likely to expose President Roosevelt's presence in the region, something that was carefully kept secret for security reasons, he dismissed the risk saying "They'd probably assume the messages had been sent from Washington, and anyway by the time the messages were translated and delivered to the addressees, we'd be at our destination."

King Farouk was President Roosevelt's guest for lunch at noon on February 13th. Emperor Haile Selassie was scheduled to board the *Quincy* that afternoon in time for tea, after King Farouk took his leave. King ibn Saud was invited to lunch the following day.

Major General Benjamin F. Giles, Commanding General of U.S. Armed Forces in the Middle East, arranged to have King Farouk and his party flown from Cairo to Deversoir Airfield adjacent to where the *Quincy* was anchored in Great Bitter Lake.

I was aboard the *Quincy* when King Farouk arrived. He was wearing a red fez and the uniform of an Egyptian admiral, the latter patterned after that of a British admiral. He was accompanied by S. Pinkney ("Pinky") Tuck, Minister at the American Legation in Cairo; Hassanein Pasha, Chief of the Royal Cabinet; and an Egyptian naval aide.

King Farouk chatted privately with the president on the deck of the *Quincy* while I photographed them. Minister Tuck and those accompanying the king were not privy to the conversation between the two leaders. The president subsequently informed the American Legation in Cairo of the essence of their conversation. He stated that he suggested to King Farouk that many of the large landed estates in Egypt be broken up and made available for ownership by the fellaheen who worked them, and that at least 100,000 additional acres be placed under irrigation annually on a continuing program.

After a pleasant luncheon, President Roosevelt had a serious talk with Hassanein Pasha, while King Farouk was guided on a tour of the ship by the captain of the *Quincy*.

On the fantail of the ship were two amphibious planes mounted on catapults. For the benefit of King Farouk, the captain arranged a demonstration to show how these aircraft were launched. It proved to be more dramatic than planned. At the captain's order, the first plane rocketed along the length of the catapult, then plunged straight into the sea. A rescue party was immediately organized. The pilot was plucked out of the water unhurt and, a few minutes later, the plane was hoisted up on deck. Then the second plane was launched successfully. There can be no doubt that King Farouk was impressed by this spectacular, but unplanned aspect of the performance.

King Farouk and his party left the USS *Quincy* at 3:00 P.M., giving the president an opportunity to rest before the arrival at 5:00 P.M. of Emperor Haile Selassie, the Lion of Judah.

Admiral Leahy met Emperor Selassie and his entourage at the airport and drove them to the port where they took a launch to the

Meeting between President Roosevelt and Selassie aboard the USS Quincy on February 13, 1945 at Great Bitter Lake on the Suez Canal.

Quincy. The Emperor, dressed in an unadorned military uniform, was accompanied by his son, a tall young man wearing a business suit. Also present was the Ethiopian Vice Minister of Finance, Ato Yilma Deressa.

After the president greeted them, they were taken on a conducted tour of the ship before taking tea with the president in his cabin. In the ensuing conversation, conducted in French, the emperor brought up the subject of Ethiopia's need for a port at Djibouti, where there is a railroad, but said that eventually it would be desirable to have one at Eritrea as well. In response to Roosevelt's question, the emperor said that it would be feasible to construct a railroad there. The president advised the emperor that if the construction were undertaken by an American company, too much should not be paid for its services. He said he would give the same advice should a petroleum pipeline be built there. But, according to Minister Tuck, the president gave the emperor no commitments, promises or assurances of any kind to his requests for assistance.

Certainly the most spectacular, exotic and significant of the three royal visits, was that of King Abdul Aziz ibn Saud of Saudi Arabia on February 14th.

President Roosevelt had sent the U.S. destroyer *Murphy* to Jidda to carry the king and his retinue to Great Bitter Lake for the meeting.

I was briefed along with others about the impending visit. We were told that no women were permitted to be on board, which meant that the president's daughter Anna had to return to Egypt prior to the arrival of the king. Moreover, it was prohibited to smoke or drink alcoholic beverages during the royal visit. We were told that the king had some 300 wives and concubines, 60 sons and uncounted daughters, and that he selected his wives from the various tribes to unite them and ensure their allegiance to him.

I was given the following list of those who would accompany the king:

Saudi Arabian Guests
February 14, 1945

His Majesty Adbul Aziz ibn Rahman al Faisal al Saud, King of Saudi Arabia.

His Royal Highness, Emir al Saud, Abdulla (brother of the king).
Shalkh Yusuf Yassin, Deputy Minister of Foreign Affairs.
His Royal Highness, Mohammed al Saud (son of the king).
His Royal Highness, Emir Mansour al Saud (son of the king).

Shalkh Abdullah Sulkayman, Minister of Finance.
Shalkh Yusuf Yassin, Deputy Minister of Foreign Affairs.
Shalkh Haviz Wahba, Minister Plenipotentiary to Great Britain.
Shalkh Bashir Saadawi, Privy Counsellor.
Doctor Rashad Far'oun, King's Physician.

Majid ibn Khathaiz (Astologer and Fortuneteller).
Abdul Rahman Djuez (Iman, chaplain who leads palace prayers)
Brigadier Sa'id Gaudet (Commander of the king's guards) Aide de Camp.
Captain Mohammed al Thelb (Adjutant of the Guards) Ass't Aide de Camp.
Sulayman Bey al Hamid (Ass't to Minister of Finance, his uncle).
Mohammed Abdul Djither (Chief Communications and Radio Officer).
Mahsoul Effendi (Adjutant of the Guards).
Sa'id Abdoul Djither (Radio Supervisor of the Najd).

Abdullah al Tuwagry (Communications Assistant).
Nutlag ibn Zaid (Palace Representative of the Mutayr tribe).
Cassab ibn Mandil (Palace Representative of the Beni Kalid tribe).
Abdullah bil Kheir (Interpreter and monitor of English broadcasts).
Sirag Dhaharan (Official food-taster and caterer).
Amin al Abdul Aziz (Chamberlain and chief valet).
Abdullah al Hadrami (Royal Purse-bearer).
Amin al Abdul Wahid (Chief Server of ceremonial coffee).
Abdul Rahman ibn Abdul Wahid (Second Server of ceremonial coffee).
10 Guards with sabres and daggers chosen from principle tribes.
3 Valets, one for each royal prince.
9 Miscellaneous slaves, cooks, porters, scullions.
48 Total

King ibn Saud had never been outside the borders of Saudi
Arabia. Consequently, when he boarded the U.S. destroyer at Jidda,
there was great consternation among his followers that he had been
kidnapped by the Americans. In the hours that followed, wild rumors
swept through Jidda concerning the presumed dire fate of their king.

When the USS *Murphy* pulled abreast of the *Quincy*, I was
astonished to see that the destroyer's decks were covered with oriental rugs. Fierce-looking Saudi warriors armed with sabres, daggers
and ancient rifles lined the starboard rail. Three royal princes stood
on the port side closest to the *Quincy,* watching the maneuvers of the
destroyer. A golden throne richly upholstered in silk had been placed
under the six-inch gun of the destroyer.

On the stern of the destroyer was a flock of sheep, the primary
source of food for Saudi Arabian bedouins. Two of the sheep had
been slaughtered on the fantail of the vessel before the ship arrived
alongside the *Quincy.*

I was told that en route to the meeting the Iman led palace
prayers for the king and his retinue five times a day after receiving
from the captain the precise compass reading toward Mecca.

The King declined the captain's offer to sleep in his cabin,
preferring to sleep under a tent which had been rigged over the six-
inch gun on the foredeck. The tent was taken down before the
Murphy came alongside the *Quincy.*

Carefully, the captain of the destroyer inched his ship closer and
closer to the cruiser, then the two were lashed together and a gangway was rigged to permit King ibn Saud to make his way from one
ship to the other. He walked very slowly, using a cane with one hand

Emperor Haile Selassie being conducted on a tour of the USS Quincy by its captain on February 13, 1945.

and holding the gangway railing with the other. When he was about halfway across, the current moved the destroyer forward and the gangway tipped precariously. I feared the king would fall in the water between the ships, but he held on stoically, then moved sedately on board the *Quincy* when the ships stabilized.

The King was dressed in a black *djelabba* trimmed in gold, and wore a red and white *kaffia* fashioned as a turban. He was a giant of a man, measuring at least six foot seven inches tall. His face was deeply tanned and he had a black moustache and a small black beard.

The president, wearing his navy cape, was seated in his wheelchair. He invited the king to sit by his side. Huge American and Saudi Arabian flags floated in the background. U.S. Marine Colonel William A. Eddy, the U.S. Minister Plenipotentiary to the Kingdom of Saudi Arabia, spoke Arabic with native fluency. He knelt on one knee on the unyielding deck in front of the two leaders and served as their interpreter throughout their conversation, which lasted over an hour.

I was busy taking pictures of them and only caught snatches of their conversation as translated by Colonel Eddy. At one point, the

King ibn Saud crossing the gangway from the USS Murphy to the USS Quincy for his meeting with President Roosevelt on February 14, 1945.

king remarked that he and the president were "twins" because they were the same age, were both rulers, and both were physically handicapped—he because of wounds to his legs inflicted in battle, and the president because he was confined to a wheelchair. I mentally flinched at this because the president's infirmity was never mentioned by an outsider.

The president responded by saying the king was luckier than he because the king could still get about on his legs, while he had to be wheeled about. "No," replied the king, "you are the more fortunate. Your wheelchair will take you wherever you want to go, but my legs are less reliable and are getting weaker every day." Roosevelt then said, "If you think so highly of this chair, I will give you its twin, as I have two on board." The order was given and the second wheelchair was immediately taken across to the *Murphy*.

The chair proved to be too small for the king's huge frame, so the president sent a message to Mrs. Roosevelt to have one large enough to accommodate him sent to the palace in Riyadh. But it was the original one that the king displayed in his private apartment in the palace. He would show it to special guests, saying, "This is my most prized possession. It was given to me by my great and good friend, President Roosevelt."

It was in the cordial atmosphere of this initial meeting that a firm friendship was established between the two leaders.

I was not present when President Roosevelt raised the subject of how to resolve the problem of the Jewish survivors of the Holocaust in Central Europe. Subsequently I learned that Roosevelt said that he felt a personal responsibility and was committed to helping solve the problem. He asked for suggestions from the king.

The King replied, "Give them and their descendants the choicest lands and homes of the Germans who oppressed them."

Roosevelt remarked that the Jewish survivors have a sentimental desire to settle in Palestine, and quite understandably would dread remaining in Germany where they might suffer again.

"No doubt the Jews have good reason not to trust the Germans," said the king, "But surely the Allies will destroy Nazi power forever and their victory will be strong enough to protect Nazi victims. If the Allies do not expect firmly to control future German policy, why fight this costly war?" The King could not conceive of leaving an enemy in a position to strike back after defeat.

Roosevelt countered by saying that he counted on Arab hospitality and on the king's help in solving the problem, but the king repeated, "Make the enemy and the oppressor pay; that is how we Arabs wage war. Amends should be made by the criminal, not by the innocent bystander. What injury have the Arabs done to the Jews of Europe? It is the 'Christian' Germans who stole their homes and lives. Let the Germans pay."

The King's final remark on the subject was to the effect that it is the Arab custom to distribute survivors and victims of battle among the victorious tribes in accordance with their number and their supplies of food and water. "In the Allied camp," he said, "there are fifty countries, among whom Palestine is small, land-poor and has already been assigned more than its quota of European refugees."

Then the king asked Roosevelt for friendship and support. He stated that his first desire for his land and his people was independence. Unlike some other Arab lands, his country had never been occupied or "protected" as a dependent. Without this independence, he would not and could not seek an honorable friendship, because friendship is possible only with mutual and equal respect.

Next to independence, the king said, came his desire for the president's friendship because President Roosevelt was known as the champion of the Four Freedoms and never colonized or enslaved. In very simple language, such as he must have used in cementing alliances with tribal chiefs, ibn Saud asked Roosevelt for his friendship.

The president gave the king his assurance that as president of the United States, he would never do anything which might prove hostile to the Arabs and that the U.S. government would make no change in its basic policy in Palestine without the full and prior consultation with both Jews and Arabs.

To the king, these oral assurances were equal to an alliance.

Before taking his leave of the president, the king had several large bundles delivered to the *Quincy*. They were unwrapped before the president and the king. They contained fabulous gifts for the president and Mrs. Roosevelt. The most important gift for the president was a magnificent sword encased in a diamond-encrusted scabbard. The sword and scabbard are now in a vault at the Franklin D. Roosevelt Library at Hyde Park and are put on display on special occasions. Other gifts included a number of full-dress harem costumes colorfully embroidered in silk and gold and several vials of Arabian perfumes contained in rare tinted glass or in alabaster containers. There were large pieces of uncut amber from the bottom of the Red Sea and pearl rings, pearl earrings, pearl-studded bracelets and anklets, as well as belts elaborately woven in gold thread. Finally, there was an array of richly-colored oriental rugs.

I was with my father and the president when they were discussing these gifts. The president was overwhelmed by the magnitude of the king's generosity. He told my father that the king particularly admired the presidential aircraft, the *Sacred Cow*, in particular because it had an elevator to lift the president into it and to lower him down when the plane landed.

"He obviously wanted me to offer it to him," said the president. "But I can't give away such an expensive gift without the authorization of Congress." When he returned to the United States, President Roosevelt arranged to have a C-47 flown to King ibn Saud as a gift. I participated in the celebration of the 50th anniversary of this historic meeting between President Roosevelt and King ibn Saud and learned that the king used this aircraft to fly him to the far-reaches of his kingdom. Later, this C-47 aircraft became the nucleus of the now-powerful Saudi Arabian commercial air fleet and it is now on display at the airport in Riyadh.

The deck of the USS Murphy, which carried King ibn Saud from Jidda to Great Bitter Lake. Note the oriental carpets on the deck, the king's golden throne, and his royal bodyguard team, composed of the most fearsome warriors in Saudi Arabia.

General "Pa" Watson was very ill and confined to the sick bay aboard the *Quincy* during the visits of the three kings. Here, three decks below in cramped quarters designed to accommodate scores of soldiers wounded in battle, he was isolated from the excitement of the royal visits. Whenever the president was secluded to meet with his royal guests, I would go down to the sick bay to visit with General Watson and describe to him the colorful and remarkable events I had witnessed. I was deeply distressed to learn that this gentle man died at sea en route back to the United States.

We headed back to Alexandria, Egypt aboard the *Quincy* after the king and his retinue took their departure for Jidda aboard the USS *Murphy*. We arrived on the morning of February 15th. Anna was waiting for us and came on board immediately. Later, Ambassador Winant and Secretary of State Stettinius arrived and the president briefed them on his visits with the three kings.

At noon, Prime Minister Churchill arrived for an informal family luncheon with the president, Anna and my father. Churchill was accompanied by his daughter Sarah and his son Randolph. After a relaxed visit, Churchill and his children went ashore. It was the last time Churchill saw the president.

We then sailed from Alexandria to Algiers. On our way, a message was received from General de Gaulle, who was refusing to meet with President Roosevelt in Algiers.

My father was worn out from the strain of the previous weeks and informed the president that he could not endure the long sea voyage home and had to take a few days rest in Morocco before flying back to Washington. He said he intended to debark in Algiers.

This irritated the president, who had been counting on Dad to help him write the speech he intended to deliver to the joint houses of Congress on his return. But Dad was adamant. I, too, was getting off at Algiers to fly back to my unit in Paris. I said goodbye to the president and thanked him for his kindness in asking me to cover the Yalta Conference and his meetings with the three kings.

Dad was in a grouchy mood as we took the launch into the port of Algiers. It was only after we arrived that Dad remembered he had not said goodbye to the president. He lamented the fact that their parting was strained. He never saw the president alive again.

My father's health had been poor at Yalta, but now he looked so frail and exhausted that I suggested he rest a few days in Algiers. He dismissed the idea, saying he would rest in Morocco. I took him to the Maison Blanche Airport for his flight to Marrakech, then caught my own flight to Paris.

After three days in Marrakech, my father flew home. His doctor took one look at him and sent him straight to the Mayo Clinic in Rochester. He remained hospitalized there for weeks.

Back in Washington, my father sent one complete set of my photographs of the Yalta Conference to my mother to hold for me until I returned from the war. Another set of prints was sent to the Franklin D. Roosevelt Library in Hyde Park, and the third set, I understand, is in the National Archives.

Before leaving Yalta, Churchill had made arrangements to meet with the three kings after Roosevelt concluded his talks with them. He flew from Yalta to Athens and then on to Cairo. There, while awaiting the end of Roosevelt's meetings with the three sovereigns, Churchill met with the president of Syria to defuse an impending crisis caused by actions of the French government threatening the independence of Syria.

King ibn Saud and President Roosevelt aboard the USS Quincy on February 14, 1945. Translating in the foreground is Colonel William Eddy, U.S. Special Representative to Saudi Arabia.

Churchill met with the three kings as he said he would. From what I have been able to learn, these were not pleasant encounters as Churchill sternly endeavored to reassert the dominant role of Great Britain in these countries. King Farouk, who bristled at British efforts to run his country, was not receptive to Churchill's visit. While I have never seen reports of Churchill's visit with Emperor Haile Selassie, I surmise that he reminded the emperor that it was the British army which restored him to the throne in 1941 after Mussolini's army invaded and occupied Ethiopia in 1933 and deposed the emperor a year later.

As we had been, Churchill was informed prior to his meeting with King ibn Saud that there was to be no smoking or alcohol in the presence of the king. Churchill employed this as his means to gain the offensive in his discussions with the king during lunch when Churchill was host. According to his own words in Volume VI of *The Second World War*, Churchill said through the interpreter, "If it is the religion of His Majesty to deprive himself of smoking and alcohol, I must point out that it is my rule of life prescribed as an absolutely sacred rite smoking cigars and also the drinking of alcohol before, after and if need be during all meals and in the intervals between then."

This was an affront of the first order, but according to Churchill, "The King graciously accepted the position." I have since talked with Saudi diplomats about this incident, and they assured me that nothing more insulting could have been said to the king.

Nevertheless, the king's gifts to Churchill were similar to those he had given to President Roosevelt. Churchill reciprocated by promising the king that the British government would present him with the finest motorcar built.

On March 10, 1945, King ibn Saud sent a long and impassioned letter to President Roosevelt. In it, the king traced the ancient history of Palestine to support his contention that Zionist claims in Palestine were not based on historical facts. President Roosevelt responded in a letter dated April 5, 1945 in which he pledged in writing to King ibn Saud that as long as he was president of the United States he would never do anything which might prove hostile to the Arabs and that the U.S. government would make no change in its basic policy in Palestine without the full and prior consultation with both Jews and Arabs.

A week later, President Roosevelt died of a cerebral hemorrhage. His successor, President Harry Truman, did not feel constrained to abide by this pledge.

President Truman's secretary of state, Jimmy Byrnes, recalled to Washington the chiefs of U.S. missions of Egypt, Lebanon, Syria, Saudi Arabia, and the Consul General to mandated Palestine to brief President Truman on the deterioration of American political interests in the Near East. But the White House advisors persuaded President Truman that it would be impolitic to meet with his representatives to Arab countries prior to the November Congressional elections.

At a press conference on October 19th, 1945, with the Congressional elections in the offing. President Truman expressed the hope that Great Britain would accept his proposal for Palestine to be opened to 100,000 displaced Jews in Germany and Austria.

The chiefs of mission were kept idle in Washington for four weeks. Only after the November elections did the meet privately with President Truman. The briefing took 20 minutes. There was little discussion and the president asked few questions. He is alleged to have summed up his position on Palestine with these words:

"I'm sorry gentlemen, but I have to answer to hundreds of thousands who are anxious for the success of Zionism; I do not have hundreds of thousands of Arabs among my constituents."

CHAPTER 15

FLYING BOMBS AND V-2 ROCKETS

I had been back in Paris only a few days before I was assigned to shoot a documentary film in Belgium and Holland to show the devastation caused to the ports of Antwerp and Rotterdam by German flying bombs and V-2 rockets. Using these awesome pilotless weapons, the Germans attacked these two port cities and London with ferocity born of desperation as the Allied armies relentlessly advanced toward Berlin.

We were supposed to be able to complete this assignment in ten days, but in fact it took almost five weeks. My partner was Sergeant Freeman ("Slim") Ingledew, an experienced cameraman who had crossed the Atlantic with me in October 1942. I was happy to be working with him.

A script had been written in advance which we were expected to follow, although we were given some latitude in the event we found some action or activity which fit into the framework of the film. It called for some interior scenes, which meant we had to take along more equipment than usual, including floodlights, reels of electric cables, a dolly, and of course ample film. Instead of a jeep, we were issued a weapons carrier, which was large enough to accommodate the equipment we needed. "Tex," the amiable burly driver who was assigned to us, handled the heavy equipment with ease.

We left Paris on March 8th, arriving in Antwerp two days later. I found us a billet in a bomb-damaged building. There was a large unoccupied room on the second floor which at least provided a roof over our heads. The glass had been blown out of all the windows and there was no electricity. There was, however, electric power in the building across the street where some British soldiers were quartered.

They obligingly agreed to let us plug into their power, so we strung a wire from their building to ours, giving us light at least. We found fabric which served as blackout curtains to cover the windows at night.

The Germans treated us to a heavy assault of flying bombs and V-2 rockets that night, the intensity of which explained why there was no glass in our windows or in any other building in the city.

I was tortured by the knowledge that these terrible weapons were raining down on London as well, and that my beloved wife, Brenda, was in jeopardy. I could not put that image out of my mind.

Tex had a severe reaction to the bombing. He was terrified, trembling and incoherent as we endured the thundering assault. I had been told in Paris that he was a "limited service" man, but I wasn't sure what that meant. After he was able to compose himself, he told us he was suffering from battle fatigue. He had already seen a great deal of combat prior to his assignment to us. Headquarters made a poor choice in sending him to Antwerp, knowing it was a city under constant bombardment.

We made no effort to film the scenario in the order that it was written, choosing instead to let the film editor put it together in the proper sequence.

First, we filmed the interiors called for in the script. These scenes were filmed in a subterranean plotting room where reports were received and plotted on a huge map table showing launchings of flying bombs, squadrons of German fighters and bombers headed for Antwerp, Rotterdam and London, and the location of British and American aircraft to intercept them. These were detected by radar and by visual observers located on the Belgium and Dutch borders with Germany. Their reports were relayed by field telephone to the plotting room. Then the alert was sounded in the target areas and at airfields where fighter planes were scrambled to intercept them. When launchings of the V-2s were spotted and reported, air raid sirens were sounded in the target cities but there was no real defense against them. They travelled so fast that those seeking shelter were caught exposed in the street when the V-2 exploded. Many people simply moved into a shelter.

We worked on these sequences for three days and nights, usually working until one o'clock in the morning. Here in the plotting room we were safe from the German aerial attacks, but when we emerged we had to seek shelter where we could.

The denizens of Antwerp seemed to have a sixth sense about the imminent silent approach of a V-2. One night when I went out to buy some bread, the doorman of a basement nightclub suddenly grabbed my arm and flung me down some steps to the door of the club with him on top of me. Here, below street level, we were protected from the tremendous explosion of a V-2 which demolished a whole block of buildings.

Tex was so agitated and jumpy from the successive attacks from flying bombs and V-2s that he was making us nervous, too. We reluctantly decided we would have to give up his services, much as we needed them. We sent him to a nice quiet country town where he remained until we returned to Paris.

We filmed the extensive damage to Antwerp and its port facilities before moving on to film radar sites and Allied pilots scrambling to intercept flying bombs. The technique developed by Spitfire pilots of the Royal Air Force was to fly so close to the flying bomb that the pilot could put the tip of his wing under that of the flying bomb, then tip it off course. This did not prevent an eventual explosion, but diverted the bomb from a sensitive target. It was a risky maneuver, but the RAF pilots became adept at it.

Colonel Popkess, in Paris, arranged for us to get the services of a bomber so we could film Antwerp and Rotterdam from the air. We filmed from the clear plastic nose of the aircraft. It was an eerie feeling of being suspended in midair, detached from anything familiar.

Back on the ground, we went on to Rotterdam, where the situation was similar to that in Antwerp. We were becoming dispirited at seeing so much death and destruction and the racket that accompanied it. But the Dutch gave us a warm welcome, inviting us into their homes where we shared our food rations with them. Most of them spoke English and were eager to hear from us about the war in other sectors.

When we finished shooting the scenes in and around Rotterdam and Dutch efforts to rebuild, we moved on to film early warning observers in Holland located on the border with Germany. Here, with powerful binoculars, they could see flying bombs and V-2 rockets as they lifted off the launching pad. They used their field telephones to alert the plotting center in Antwerp and Allied air bases to intercept them.

It was a beautiful sunny spring day when we set up to film these scenes in a field behind a Dutch convent. We were filming a flight of three flying bombs headed our way when the engine on one stopped. We knew we had just 30 seconds to find shelter, so we left our camera running, and hastily sought cover. The bomb came down and exploded in the field some distance from us. Its concussion neatly ripped the roof shingles off as if they were playing cards.

In a matter of minutes the nuns emerged from the convent to survey the damage. We kept the camera rolling as some of them gathered up the shingles in baskets, while other erected ladders against the eaves. After fastening up their voluminous skirts, they clambered up the ladders, each carrying a basket of shingles, a hammer and nails and began to replace the roof. I could not but admire their spunk.

This sequence completed our film and provided an upbeat ending to it. We loaded up our equipment, picked up Tex and drove back to Paris, relieved that this assignment was over.

We arrived in Paris on April 12th. The war seemed far away and I felt the tension of the previous weeks ease away as I walked toward headquarters in the warm morning sun. There I received the good news that my commission as a second lieutenant had been approved. I was to be discharged from the army on April 20th, enjoy 24 hours as a civilian, and then be formally commissioned as an officer on the 21st.

CHAPTER 16

A HERO DIES

little after midnight, in the early morning hours of April
13, 1945, I heard the stunning news on the radio that
President Roosevelt had died the previous day. The president, my friend, was dead. I said it over and over to myself, trying to
impress this terrible fact on my consciousness. He and Mrs.
Roosevelt had made me feel welcome to visit them and my father in
the White House whenever I was free to do so. By including me as a
member of his official party at the wartime conferences, the president
helped shape my destiny. I felt an awful emptiness at his demise.

In the days that followed I became aware that the French
people on the street were as stricken as I. Some, strangers to me,
came with tears in their eyes to offer me condolences, not because I
knew the president, but simply because I was an American soldier to
whom they felt the need to express their sorrow.

I wrote a long letter to my father, who was again hospitalized at
the Mayo Clinic, knowing how deeply he must be affected. I also
wrote to Mrs. Roosevelt to try to comfort her in her loss. Because my
father was so ill, I tried to spur him on to recovery, writing in part:

*I know how you must feel Dad, and you know how I feel about it.
But you must take care of yourself. I think I know as well as anyone how
much you did to help the President. Now your counsel will be needed more
than ever to help President Truman. You are the only one who knows all
the plans the President had for foreign and domestic policies during and
after the war. Everyone looks to you, as President Roosevelt's friend and
advisor, to carry on in that capacity with President Truman. But you
must take care of yourself.*

Dad replied by cable, which read:

THE NEWS IS A TERRIBLE SHOCK AND, AS YOU WELL
KNOW, I HAVE LOST MY GREATEST FRIEND BUT IT IS
OF FAR GREATER IMPORTANCE THAT THE POOR AND
IMPOVERISHED OF THE WORLD HAVE LOST THEIR
GREATEST CHAMPION AND THE HOPE OF A JUST
PEACE HAS BEEN GRIEVOUSLY WOUNDED. I AM LEAV-
ING ROCHESTER THIS MORNING TO ATTEND THE
SERVICES BUT WILL RETURN HERE TO FINISH THE
BUSINESS WHICH SHOULD NOT TAKE TOO LONG
NOW.
                                LOVE, DAD.

A week passed, somehow. Newspapers and magazines in Paris
were full of the photographs I took at Yalta and at the meetings with
the three kings. As an official army photographer, I received no
personal credit for the films I made or the photographs I took, and
they were often incorrectly credited to commercial news organizations. It was gratifying to see them, however, because I rarely saw the
product of my labors while I was overseas. At the same time, the
photos reminded me of what the world had just lost.

On April 21st, officers from the Photo GHQ of the 3908th
Signal Service Battalion were there to welcome me to their ranks. In
a curious ceremony, my commanding officer dropped the gold bars of
my rank into a glass of cognac and said I must drink the cognac
without swallowing the gold bars. With some difficulty, I downed
the cognac, straining the fiery liquid between my teeth. Then, my
gold bars were pinned to my epaulets and I was congratulated by the
men who were now my fellow officers. One of the officers there who
served on the commissioning board told me that the board was
unaware that my father was Harry Hopkins. This pleased me because
it meant that I had received the commission on my own merits.

Before leaving, they reminded me that I must pay a dollar to
the first soldier who salutes me, which I did to the sentry posted
outside the building. That night they gave a party in my honor for
having risen to the rank of officer in the United States Army.

It was the next day that I received orders to report to London,
as Assignments Officer for the photo unit covering the entire United
Kingdom. I couldn't have received better news.

CHAPTER 17

RETURN TO ENGLAND AND WAR'S END

Before leaving Paris, I went to our lab to say goodbye to my friends there. They were in the process of printing the horrifying photographs of the atrocities at Auschwitz which had been shot by one of our photographic teams. The pictures showed the bodies of gaunt men, women and children stacked like cord wood. The survivors looked like walking skeletons with haunted eyes.

Later I learned that millions of Jews, Gypsies and homosexuals had been incarcerated there and in other concentration camps where some had been subjected to atrocious medical experiments. Others were tortured, executed by poison gas or worked to death as slaves.

No words could describe it. Only the photographs could effectively attest to this Nazi infamy.

I said goodbye to my colleagues and the friends I had made in Paris, including Marie-Louise Bousquet, promising her I would return one day with Brenda. I then flew to London and into Brenda's arms.

The war in Europe was unraveling quickly. On May 1st, Hitler committed suicide, and Berlin fell to Russian troops the next day.

Then, on May 7th, Admiral Doenitz signed Germany's unconditional surrender.

Now that victory in Europe had finally arrived, everyone felt a tremendous sense of relief, but I found that few were especially elated, knowing that the war in the Pacific was far from over.

Brenda and I visited Lord Beaverbrook. He was pleased to see us together again and we had a good talk, but our visit was necessarily short because both he and I had to make preparations for the Victory in Europe celebrations.

Church bells pealed all over London and throughout England. Tens of thousands of people swarmed into the streets in jubilation. I and all the photographers and cameramen under my command turned out to photograph and film the celebration that went on all day and night. The City of London tried to turn on the streetlights which had been off since the beginning of the Blitz, but birds had built their nests in them and the lights did not go on again as Londoners fervently hoped they would. But blackout curtains came down and lights appeared in the windows of the city. The good-natured crowd was so dense in Picadilly Circus that people moved only as the mass of humanity surged in one direction or another.

After the initial euphoria faded, Churchill declared that rationing of food and clothing must continue, and grim reality set in.

General Eisenhower announced in the newspaper *Stars and Stripes* that he was anxious that no combat soldier be sent to the Pacific who had fought in both North Africa and Europe. This was a great relief to me. I had seen enough combat and was not looking forward to spending another two or three years in the war against the Japanese.

There was an acute housing shortage in London, as we discovered when we endeavored to find a flat in the city where we could be on our own. Pamela Churchill told me about a flat that was available in Grosvenor Square. It was beautiful but much too big and costly for my modest salary as a second lieutenant. We resigned ourselves to accepting the offer from Brenda's parents to move into what had been Brenda's bedroom at their house in Perivale. All that really mattered, after all, was that Brenda and I were together.

We would ride to work on the train and the metro every morning, Brenda to her job with the U.S. Army Chaplains' Office in Grosvenor Square and I to our photo headquarters two blocks away on Davies Street. We would meet daily for lunch, which we ate quickly, then stroll through London's ancient streets looking at antique shops before returning to work. On weekends we went on rambles organized by the Red Cross, or on occasion we would visit with Lord Beaverbrook at his country home.

Because Brenda had married a foreigner, the British government took away her citizenship, the English version of a slap on the wrist. Then the government tried to tax her on her American income from the army. Brenda pointed out to government bureaucrats that

President Harry Truman's meeting with King George VI at Portsmouth aboard the HMS Ronown, immediately after the Potsdam Conference.

since she was no longer a British citizen and her income was derived only in dollars from American army sources, she was not subject to British income tax. The British government backed down.

Unlike my mother when she married my father in 1913, Brenda did not automatically become an American citizen when we married. She was stateless until she passed her naturalization examination and became an American citizen.

These were halcyon days for us. The bombings had stopped and the lights were on again. Brenda had gone through the inferno of the Blitz on London. Then she was frequently in more danger from the

Germans than I, but now the Germans had capitulated. The night-mare was over and we were together again.

We began to spruce up Brenda's room. We painted the walls, stained the floor and refinished the furniture. The room was now much brighter, more cheerful and seemed larger than before.

I was kept busy with my new responsibilities but I could not help but think about what I would do when I was demobilized and had to earn a living in a civilian world. It occurred to me that I might be able to organize a civilian pictorial service, bringing in with me photographers and cameramen who I knew to be skilled and depend-able. I began to sound out some of the men about this. They seemed interested.

The army released a point system as a means of determining when soldiers would be sent back to the United States for discharge. The first to return to the States would be those with 85 points. I had 100 points, based on length of service abroad. But there was a catch—ships were not permitted to carry war brides to America until all the soldiers had returned. I had no desire to leave Brenda and was content to remain with her in England.

In June, a conference was held in San Francisco to formalize the United Nations Organization as approved by Roosevelt, Churchill and Stalin at Yalta. Almost immediately disputes arose over which countries should be members of the Security Council. Molotov wanted to bring in the Ukraine and two other countries in the Soviet orbit, which would tip the balance in favor of Russia in all debates. The composition of the postwar Polish government was also a matter of bitter disagreement. The stalemate threatened the future of the United Nations. To dramatize the situation, Molotov walked out of the conference and flew back to Moscow.

Alarmed at the risk of collapse of the United Nations, Chip Bohlen suggested to Averell Harriman, who was then Ambassador to Russia, that President Truman might consider sending my father to Moscow to resolve the problem in direct talks with Stalin.

My father had retired from the government following the death of President Roosevelt and was recuperating at his house in Georgetown. Together, Chip and Averell proposed the idea to Dad, who although weak and ill, expressed his enthusiasm at the prospect but said he was sure Truman would not go along with it.

Truman hesitated in view of Dad's fragile health, but decided to ask him if he felt well enough to do it. Dad replied immediately in the affirmative. After being briefed by the president, Dad flew to

Moscow. In a series of intense discussions with Stalin, my father broke the deadlock and the United Nations was saved.

I didn't attend the Potsdam Conference, but I did go to Plymouth immediately afterward to photograph President Truman's meeting with King George VI aboard the HMS *Renown*.

As soon as President Truman got out of his car, he came straight over to me and shook hands. I was startled because I had never met him before. I began to introduce myself, but he interrupted me, saying "I *know* who you are!" Someone must have pointed me out to him. I was flattered by his attention. We chatted for a few minutes about Dad and he expressed his admiration for all that my father had done for the nation. I talked to other members of the party who I knew, including Judge Sam Rosenman, Admiral Leahy, Jimmy Byrnes and several others. They all told me that Dad was feeling very low after his trip to Russia, but when they last saw him he was looking much more rested.

The United States dropped atomic bombs on Hiroshima and Nagasaki on August 6th and August 9th bringing the war against Japan to an abrupt halt. Victory over Japan, VJ-Day, prompted another popular celebration, which my men and I covered. At one point I climbed to the roof of the Law Courts across from St. Paul's Cathedral. They had been heavily bombed and the tiles on the roof were loose. Clinging precariously to a chimney pot, I photographed the elderly Queen Mary, widow of George V, as she entered the Cathedral flanked by Beefeater guards to attend the Thanksgiving services there marking the end of World War II.

The first 85 pointers shipped out of Southampton aboard the *Queen Elizabeth* for demobilization on August 24th. I realized that because I had been overseas for such a long time, I might be ordered to leave without Brenda. I checked with the transportation office and discovered that the rule prohibiting war brides from traveling to the U.S. was being strictly enforced. I then went to the air force and found that the same prohibition applied to the air force and that available space on every plane flying to the United States was filled with returning troops. Finally, in mid-September, I went to commercial airlines. Here, I was told that occasionally there was space available, but the fare was $880, which I couldn't really afford and still have money to live on in America. I turned to Ambassador Winant for help but there was little he could do.

On September 4, 1945, President Truman awarded my father the Distinguished Service Medal, then the highest award the War Department could confer on a civilian. The text is worth repeating here:

Mr. Harry L. Hopkins performed services of outstanding value to the United States of America from December 1941 to July 1945. As Special Advisor to the President during critical months of World War II, he assumed tasks of utmost urgency and far-reaching consequences, lightening the burden of the Commander-in-Chief. He gave great assistance to the armed forces in their relationships with the Chief Executive, attacking with piercing understanding the tremendous problems incident to the vast military operations throughout the world. As Chairman of the Munitions Assignment Board, he channeled material to all Allied force with a skill measurable in terms of the steady successes which have been achieved in crushing Germany and closing with Japan in the final struggle. As Chairman of the President's Soviet Protocol Committee, he determined supply quotas to be dispatched to Russia, accomplishing this mission with statesmanshiplike skill. At major conferences with world powers he threw his every effort toward the speedy solution to weighty problems. With deep appreciation of the armed forces' needs and broad understanding of the Commander-in-Chief's over-all policy, with exceptional ability to weld our Allies to the common purpose of victory over aggression, Mr. Hopkins made a selfless, courageous and objective contribution to the war effort.

When Dad commented to me about this in a letter dated September 19, 1945, he wrote, "You probably have read in the papers that Truman gave me the Distinguished Service Medal. Naturally I am pleased but, of course, there are many others who deserve it quite as much."

Meanwhile, Dad, Louise and Diana moved from their house in the Georgetown section of Washington to New York City and rented a house at 1046 Fifth Avenue. Dad had decided to write a book about his government service and had moved 40 file cabinets containing his official and personal papers into the house. He hired Sidney Hyman, who had been a classmate of my older brother David at the University of Chicago, to help sort the papers for him.

Then, at the end of September, I received orders to report to Southampton to board *the Queen Elizabeth* bound for New York. There was no way I could postpone this departure, nor could I devise

Queen Mary, the widow of King George V, ascending the steps of St. Paul's Cathedral to attend the Thanksgiving Service marking the end of World War II.

a way for Brenda to get to America so we could be together. She went with me to Southampton and we had one last night together before our wrenching separation. She returned to London as I boarded that immense ship.

The ship was jammed full with returning soldiers and officers. I was told there were 12,000 troops on board. I was assigned to a cabin which in peacetime was designed for two people. There were sixteen of us in it. There were four stacks of bunks, each four bunks high. I was the last to arrive, so I slept in a top bunk, just under the ceiling.

It was almost impossible to move through the crowded corridors of the ship and the best solution was to get out of the cabin and into one of the spacious common rooms. Fortunately the voyage lasted only five days, and I managed to get out on deck to see the Statue of Liberty and the misty skyline of Manhattan at dawn as we steamed into port on October 4, 1945.

There was a banner on the wharf reading "Welcome Home GIs!" but there was no brass band to greet us on that damp morning. It seemed to take forever for us to debark. Red Cross workers were at the foot of the gangplank to welcome us with hot coffee, doughnuts and sandwiches. Then we were trucked out to Fort Slocum for demobilization. I was urged to remain in the army so that some needed dental work could be taken care of, but I had enough experience with army dentists to decline the offer. I was told that it would take about a week before I could be discharged unless I joined the Army Reserve. Eager to get out, I joined the Reserve and was released that very day, October 4th, almost exactly four years after I joined the army.

My mother was there to meet me. She had come from California where she served in the Red Cross at the Veterans' Hospital in Pasadena.

We moved into the Essex House on Central Park South until I could get my bearings. We talked all day long and into the night about the loss of Stephen and I told her everything about Brenda, and what I could not write about during the war. Mother told me that David had been demobilized and had gone to work at Enterprise Studios as a film producer in Hollywood.

On October 18th, I received the following cable from Lord Beaverbrook:

ROBERT HOPKINS ESSEX HOUSE NEW YORK HAVE SEEN BRENDA THIS EVENING SHE LOOKS MORE BEAUTIFUL AND MORE LOVELY THAN EVER BEFORE **STOP** SHE WANTS VERY MUCH TO GET OVER AND UNLESS YOU GET HER THERE SOON SHE WILL GROW GREY HAIRS **STOP** TELL YOUR FATHER THAT IF HE SENDS A TELEGRAM TO MINISTER OF CIVIL AVIATION I SHOULD THINK HE WILL GET EVERYTHING HE WANTS **STOP** IF THIS GOVERNMENT GAVE HIM OUR ENTIRE AIRCRAFT FLEET WE SHOULD BE MAKING A VERY POOR RETURN TO HIM **STOP** WITH GREAT GOOD WISHES.

BEAVERBROOK

When I saw my father in his new home, he looked so terribly thin that my heart contracted. But he was enthusiastic about the book he intended to write and I could see that the energy within him still burned brightly.

I showed him the cable from Beaverbrook. I told him how desperate I was to get Brenda to America. He said that since he was no longer in the government, he would see what he could do to help.

He was as good as his word. He contacted Lord Halifax, the British Ambassador in Washington, who brought the matter up with Prime Minister Clement Atlee. The prime minister replied to Lord Halifax in a message dated November 8, 1945 which read:

> *I have gone into this very carefully but much as I would like to I do not see how I can help. I cannot claim that her journey is "necessary in the national interest" which is the only grounds on which we can sponsor such a passage. Secondly there has as you know been considerable agitation here about the thousands of G.I. wives whose transport we have repeatedly stated to be the responsibility of the American Military Authorities. It seems to me that to give Mrs. Hopkins a favour would be very embarrassing to the American Authorities and ourselves and this would apply particularly if she came in my party, a fact we could not keep secret.*
>
> *I'm sure Harry should get in touch with Winant and there should be no difficulty in Mrs. Robert Hopkins getting a passage in an American aircraft, provided she applies to the right quarter and is prepared to pay.*

It was a valiant effort on Dad's part, but it failed.

Discouraged at our inability to bring Brenda to me, I threw myself into the project to form a civilian pictorial service. Before leaving London I had secured the participation of five top flight army photographers who were also skilled in motion picture work. I also negotiated a contract with the director and founder of Keystone Pictures, who would handle distribution of our pictures.

In New York I looked for a building to house our enterprise. I found a three-story house on 53rd Street between Lexington and Third Avenues which could accommodate our studio, our laboratory and our offices. It had even had an apartment where Brenda and I could live. It was for sale for $52,000.

Then I got a call from David in Hollywood. He told me he had encountered Darryl Zanuck who was expecting a telephone call from me. I had completely forgotten that Zanuck had asked me to call him when I was demobilized. David gave me the telephone number and I placed the call. Zanuck said he wanted me to come out to Hollywood to work for him at 20th Century Fox Films in the field of production. He said I could name my own price. I asked if I could think about it for a couple of days. He said to call him on Wednesday with my decision.

I contacted Hugh Rennie, a long-time friend of mine. He and his wife, Dorthea Duckworth, had acted in a number of films in Hollywood. I needed their advice on how much salary I should stipulate. I knew it should be much more that I earned at *The March of Time* before the war and more than my army salary as a second lieutenant of $125 a month. Hugh said that under the circumstances, I could ask for much more than that. After a good deal of soul-searching I selected a figure I thought to be outrageously high, called Zanuck as promised, and he immediately concurred. He asked me to get to California as soon as I could.

I informed my colleagues in the pictorial project that I would have to turn the project over to them to pursue without my participation. We parted on friendly terms.

David called to say that his wife, Cherry, was ill and he asked Mother to return to California to help out. Mother was in a quandary. She wanted to be here when Brenda arrived, but when I told her I had no way of knowing when that would be, she agreed to return to California.

Then, by a miracle, Brenda was informed that there was space available on a flight to New York arriving on December 12th, two days before her birthday. I went to the airport to meet her. I saw her emerge with the other passengers. She looked right at me, but then looked away. She didn't recognize me. She had never seen me in civilian clothes. I hurried over to her and she saw who I was and we embraced.

We held one another close in the taxi to the city and vowed never to be separated again. Brenda surmised that Lord Beaverbrook was somehow involved in finding an available seat on the airplane. She paid the fare out of our joint account, with additional financial help from her father.

Brenda was overwhelmed by the lights of New York City and by our suite at the Essex House overlooking Central Park. She was amazed at how plentiful food was in the shops—heaps of oranges, bananas and other fruits, and eggs sold by the dozen—food she hadn't seen since the beginning of the war, and all of it unrationed.

I took her to meet my uncles, Ben and Ed Gross, and they welcomed her warmly. Mimi, Ben's wife, took Brenda on a shopping spree for clothes. Together, Brenda and I went to my father's house where Brenda met Louise and Diana for the first time.

2nd Lt. Robert Hopkins celebrating his demobilization from the U.S. Army on October 4, 1945, with Irving Berlin at the Stork Club in New York City.

Then, Dad's health took a turn for the worse and he was rushed to Memorial Hospital on the East Side. We visited him every day, but I could see his strength waning. Nothing the doctors could do seemed to help him. He kept a portable radio on his bed and listened to the news to try to keep up with unfolding developments in the world. He still smoked incessantly.

Desperate, I went out to the public telephone in the hall and called President Truman in the White House. I told him about Dad's condition and asked if he could send him on another mission to rally his strength and energy, as occurred when he sent him on his last mission to Russia. The president was sympathetic but said, "Robert, I can't do that without first talking to his doctors." He said he would call me back after talking to them. An hour later he called and told me that the doctors informed him that my father was not in the condition to travel anywhere.

I returned to my father's room. I told him about Zanuck's offer and he urged me to leave right away rather than risk losing this golden opportunity. He said how pleased he was that Brenda was with me at last and that he would keep in touch with me.

Brenda and I decided to buy a used car and drive across the United States to California. We took leave of my father, Louise and Diana, and of my uncles, their wives and children. Then we headed west on Route 66.

It took us ten days to get to California. I went to 20th Century Fox Studios in Westwood and met with Darryl Zanuck who told me I would be working under Louis de Rochemont again, this time as a screen writer. I signed a contract, then Brenda and I went out house hunting. We found a lovely Spanish-style hillside house in one of the canyons in Beverly Hills. My salary at Fox was enough to qualify me for a first mortgage and we bought the house, the first home of our own. After paying the settlement fees, we had just $22 in our bank account. A few days after settlement, on January 29, 1946, my father died, not from cancer as many people thought, but of hemochromatosis, a blood disease that inhibits the assimilation of nutrients. He was only 55 years old.

This closed the first phase of my career. I was 24 years old, reunited with what remained of my immediate family, and married and happy with my wife Brenda at my side.

As to the rest of my career, Winston Churchill said it best in another context:

"This is not the end. This is not even the beginning of the end, but it is, perhaps, the end of the beginning."

CHAPTER 18

TODAY

After four years at 20th Centruy Fox, Robert went to work with the Marshall Plan in Paris as a producer of documentary radio programs describing the accomplishments of this vast economic program. In this endeavor, he worked closely with his friend, Ambassador Averell Harriman.

When the Marshall Plan ended, Robert spent two years traveling through France with Brenda while writing a guide book to France for Fodor's.

During the Cold War, with good command of French and broad international contacts, he applied for a job with the CIA. He was accepted and was active in Europe, South America, and Washington, DC. He retired from the CIA in 1980.

After his retirement from government service, Robert worked for several years as a political consultant for Transnational Executive Service, which had commercial clients with large business interests and investments. He is currently president of the Harry Hopkins Public Service Institute, a nonprofit organization designed to focus attention on the kind of dedicated public service personified by his father.

Brenda and Robert had one son, Sean, who was born in Buenos Aires in 1964. He died 26 years later of complications from AIDS. Robert wrote a book about his son's life and his ordeal with AIDS, entitled *Sean's Legacy: An AIDS Awakening*, which was published by Triumph Books in 1996.

Brenda was actively involved in raising funds for AIDS research. She passed away in January 2002, after 58 years of marriage to Robert. Robert still resides in their long-time home in Washington, DC, where he is writing a book about Brenda's life.

APPENDIX

MORE INFORMATION

Robert Hopkins was interviewed for a recent video, "Allies at War," produced by PBS affiliate WNET in Boston. Several of the stories and photos featured in this book are also featured in the video.

To order a copy of the video, please contact the distributor, MPI Media, through their website at www.mpimedia.com, or by phone at 708-460-0555. MPI can be reached by mail at:

MPI Media Group
16101 S. 108th Ave.
Orland Park, IL 60467

To order copies of this book for classroom use, please contact the publisher at the following address or by email at info@castlepacific.com:

Castle Pacific Publishing Company
1301 5th Avenue
Seattle, WA 98101
Toll-free 1-888-756-BOOK (2665)
www.castlepacific.com